Books and Beyond

Books and Beyond

New Ways to Reach Readers

Michael F. Opitz
Michael P. Ford
with
Matthew D. Zbaracki

HEINEMANN
Portsmouth, NH

Heinemann
A division of Reed Elsevier Inc.
361 Hanover Street
Portsmouth, NH 03801–3912
www.heinemann.com

Offices and agents throughout the world

The authors and publisher wish to thank those who have generously given
permission to reprint borrowed material:

Figure 1.5: "Text Structures" chart from the Florida Online Reading
Professional Website. Used with permission of the Just Read, Florida!
Office, Florida Department of Education.

Library of Congress Cataloging-in-Publication Data
Opitz, Michael F.
   Books and beyond : new ways to reach readers / Michael F. Opitz and
Michael P. Ford ; with Matthew D. Zbaracki.
      p. cm.
   Includes bibliographical references and index.
   ISBN-13: 978-0-325-00743-4
   ISBN-10: 0-325-00743-8
   1. Reading (Elementary).   I. Ford, Michael P.   II. Zbaracki, Matthew D.
III. Title.

LB1573.O65 2006
372.41—dc22   2006019536

Editor: Lois Bridges
Production: Vicki Kasabian
Cover design: Catherine Hawkes, Cat & Mouse Design
Typesetter: Technologies 'N Typography, Inc.
Manufacturing: Louise Richardson

Printed in the United States of America on acid-free paper
10 09 08 07 06 ML 1 2 3 4 5

While this book bears our names, it represents the work of several individuals. First is our editor, Lois Bridges, who offered timely feedback and helpful suggestions, encouragement, and enthusiasm. Then there is Vicki Kasabian, our production editor, who transformed the original manuscript into the book you see here. Next is Beth Tripp, our copy editor. This book is proof enough that she worked her magic with a sentence or two. Catherine Hawkes designed the meaningful and colorful cover. Eric Chalek rounds out the list; he chose the perfect words to capture the essence of the book on the back cover.

From Michael Opitz

I am grateful to several individuals who contributed to the manuscript in important ways: the many readers who showed me the many texts they read; the many teachers who encouraged me to write more about multilevel texts; my colleague Roger Eldridge Jr., who helped me better understand that the value in children's literature is in helping to motivate children to read; my wife, Sheryl, who took care of the day-to-day details so that I could focus on writing; and Lois Bridges, for her keen insight and for helping me to grow as a writer. To all, I offer my sincere thanks.

From Michael Ford

I would like to acknowledge the work of the many Wisconsin educators who influenced my thinking as I wrote this book, especially Kathy Buss, Stacy

Clark, Nancy Decker, Mary Jett, Lee Karnowski, Mary Kreul, Joan Larson, Lauren Leslie, Shirwill Lukes, Wayne Otto, Cheri Polster, and Janice Strop. I appreciate the support of my colleagues from the University of Wisconsin Oshkosh, especially those working side by side with me in the dean's office— you make my daily work so enjoyable. A project like this could never have been possible without the ongoing support and understanding of my family; thanks to Pat, Vo, and Pasha. Finally, a special thanks to our editor, Lois Bridges. It was great "going on the cruise" with you!

From Matthew Zbaracki

I'd like to thank my family for all of their support. Thanks to Jane for listening to the ideas and helping frame things as well. Another thank-you goes to my colleagues both at the University of Northern Colorado and across the country. Finally, a big thanks to my coauthors, Michael Opitz (FM) and Mike Ford; it's been a great process.

The catalyst for this book surfaced in places far removed from classroom reading programs. Each of us has become increasingly aware of the potential and power of alternative texts by carefully observing real readers in real contexts. Let us share three stories as a way of illustrating what we have learned.

Opitz's Story

The airport can be a place of study and it's a good thing because I frequently find myself in one on my way to consult with a wide array of educators on different aspects of reading and the other language arts. In fact, it was travel that got me to thinking about the different types of texts individuals read outside of school. An informal look around any terminal shows several types of reading preferences: fiction, nonfiction, hardcover books, softcover books, magazines, newspapers, instruction manuals, cyber texts, brochures, menus, and the list goes on.

And if you think that I watch only what adults read, think again. I watch children, too, and notice that they read all of the above. Just a couple of weeks ago, for example, I was in an airport bookstore and overheard a youngster talking to his father about a magazine. In an "I hit the jackpot" voice, the boy exclaimed, "They have it, Dad!" The father looked to see what his son was talking about and, noticing the magazine in his son's hand, smiled and nodded yes. This must have been a secret code, for without asking, the son brought the magazine to his father, who eventually paid for it. As luck would have it, the two were on my scheduled flight, so I was able to spy on the boy while we were waiting to board. Was he really *that* excited about the magazine? Would he *really* read it? My questions were soon answered.

But *devour* would be a more appropriate word than *read* because that is just how the boy went about consuming the magazine.

Ford's Story

As the father of two middle school boys, I have had many *aha* moments about readers and reading while riding in our family van. For example, one day as I was driving with my two boys in the back, one of my sons asked: "What does *exceeds capacity* mean?" I looked in the rearview mirror to see him struggling to learn how to play a new game on his Game Boy based on the Yu-Gi-Oh! playing cards. I seized the teachable moment to introduce a little vocabulary, but my son soon informed me that my advice was wrong. He then grabbed a little directions manual that came with his game. This little book was forty-two pages long and about two square inches in size. He flipped through the book repeatedly, independently trying to solve this vocabulary dilemma that was precluding him from moving forward to play his new game. He finally discovered how he was exceeding capacity and adjusted his actions so that he could proceed.

I was struck by his ability to self-direct his problem solving in such a strategic way using this small directions manual. It seemed like such a contrast to other moments I'd seen while he was doing homework. The same level of engagement, independence, and strategic problem solving often seemed missing when he was completing response questions to a novel being read in class. It made me wonder what might happen if we expanded our view and use of alternative texts in reading programs. If my two boys have taught me anything, it is that the same text won't necessarily appeal to all readers. That suggests if we are working with many different readers, we probably need to consider using many different texts.

Zbaracki's Story

Recently while I was in my parents' basement cleaning out all of the boxes containing my childhood belongings, I encountered a personal experience with many texts. As I went through the boxes, I found three separate reminders of the many texts I read as a child.

The first was my old baseball cards. Being quite careful as I pulled them out, I enjoyed looking through all the players I had collected through the years. As I flipped them over, I realized that I'm no longer as fluent as I once was in reading them. It took me a few minutes to decipher some of the stats I used to know by heart. This first experience in the basement was just the beginning, however.

I then opened another box and found my old Dungeons and Dragons manual, another text that my friends and I had read many times over. The memories of so much vocabulary—hit points, formulas, dexterity, and eight-sided dice—came rushing back. It was the last box, however, that kept me in the basement for a few more hours.

With great anticipation, I pulled the lid back from the final box, wondering what lay beneath. Inside, I found my old comic books. Archie and his pals and some other adventure comics saw the light of day for the first time in years. Poring through each booklet, I read them yet again, smiling, laughing, and remembering the fun I'd had in reading them the first time. Each of the three boxes made me realize I owed my parents a big thank-you. As I was growing up, they saw each of the different forms of text that I was reading. As I passed through each phase of text, they understood the excitement and passion I had for each new genre. Never did they tell me not to read them or that I should focus solely on books. To them, I am grateful for the first lesson about how many readers read many texts.

These experiences have led us to think once again about the types of reading materials we do and don't use in school to help children develop into lifelong readers. Books are often revered over other text types as the primary way to help children maximize their full reading potential. But when we think of the many different types of text we see children and adults read, and when we think about how many forms of print we are called on to use in the present day and age, we realize that we must go beyond books if we are truly interested in helping children become proficient readers. Like Pearson and Raphael, we believe that "neither high-quality trade books nor practice books can serve as the sole diet of books for young readers to become proficient in literacy activities" (2003, 33). In fact, we argue that this holds true for all readers, young and old alike.

But how do we as teachers go about using a variety of text types in school and still accomplish the goals of any given reading program? How do we become knowledgeable about these different texts and how we can access them? The purpose of this book is to answer questions such as these. We aim to show as much as tell just how many different text types can be used and to provide busy teachers with a handy reference for locating several different types of text.

In Chapter 1, we provide the rationale for this book. We list research-based reasons for using many different text types as well as explain the complex interaction between the text and the reader. We also offer our view of what it means to be a reader. Without a doubt, both the students and the contexts in which we teach are complicated.

In Chapters 2 through 11, we address different text types, explaining what they are and how they can be used in primary and intermediate-grade classrooms. We address everything from using magazines to using real-life texts such as Game Boy manuals. Each chapter follows the same format. We begin with a brief description of the text the given chapter showcases. Second, we present reasons for using the text. Third, we explain how the text can be used. Specific scenarios (one geared toward the primary grades, the other toward the intermediate grades) follow this explanation. Fourth, we list sample representative titles, conclusions, and useful websites.

In Chapter 12, the final chapter, we offer a classroom vignette, which features Virginia and her students using many different texts. We encourage those conducting book study groups or staff development sessions to have participants read this chapter first (thus the title, "The Last Part First") and brainstorm a list of the different texts they notice. Participants can then read this book in one of several ways and return to the vignette and the original brainstorming list to make any necessary additions to or deletions from that list. We also provide sample questions that can guide discussion and a self-assessment grid that teachers can use to determine the texts they currently have their students use during the school day (see Appendixes A and B).

Writing this book has helped us further clarify for ourselves the value of honoring all text types rather than letting one (i.e., books) reign supreme. We invite you to do the same.

CHAPTER 1

The Case for Going Beyond Books

"He's so unmotivated!" a parent responds when asked what she thinks about her son's reading. "I mean," she continues, "we subscribe to a book club and he gets one book nearly every two weeks. He'll sometimes glance through them, but he sure doesn't read them cover to cover."

Comments such as these from well-meaning parents are common. They realize that their children aren't reading books. When they try to do something about it, they often become frustrated. "After all, we read a lot in our home. Why won't he?"

Often we harbor a romantic view of what it means to be a reader. We may envision *reading* as people gathered in a group reviewing and discussing the "great" books. When a young reader doesn't match that vision, families and educators often wonder why he isn't reading. Often, the answer is simple: The child *is* reading! It may be that the child avoids books yet spends a lot of time on the computer reading about a wide array of different topics.

We all have stories from our personal lives that illustrate this point. As Michael Opitz was preparing a presentation for a group of teachers, his son remarked, "Don't you think it's interesting that those guys want your ideas about teaching reading when you have a son who doesn't read?" Fortunately, dad had enough sense to agree with his son rather than squelch his reading altogether. Little did the son realize that he was a voracious reader of some types of texts, but he defined reading exclusively as book reading. Likewise, Michael Ford's sons rarely self-select books to read as a free-time activity, which disappoints Michael and his wife, Pat, who are both reading teachers. On the other hand, Michael and Pat are delighted with the range of self-selected texts their sons do read and take heart as they watch their boys seek out and dive into magazines on topics from street racing to video gaming. Matthew Zbaracki remembered the wide variety of texts he read growing up. These included books, baseball cards, and *Dungeons and Dragons* manuals.

We have discovered that defining *reading* as *reading books* is a common misconception among adults and children alike. For this reason, we open the chapter with a definition of *text* and examine the implications for instruction. We then provide six critical reasons for using a variety of texts in classroom reading programs.

Defining Text

In *The Literacy Dictionary*, Harris and Hodges offer seven definitions of *text*. The primary definition is "the entirety of a linguistic communication, as a conversation and its situation context" (1995, 255). The remaining definitions relate to written or spoken words available for description or analysis, with a distinction made between internal and external texts. *Internal* refers to the author's words; *external* refers to the meaning of the author's words as constructed by the reader.

When we use the word *text* in this book, we are primarily focused on communication in a written form and the context in which it is presented. We are referring to the internal text, or the author's words, though we acknowledge that it is hard to divorce that discussion from the external texts created by readers. In the time that has passed since the last edition of the *Literacy Dictionary*, the definitions of *text* have continued to be rooted in words, with virtually no attention to images. As literacy standards are broadened to incorporate critical viewing, however, we want to acknowledge the importance of other texts that are often read in nontraditional ways (e.g., movies, television, and video games). While we focus mostly on word-based texts in this book, we realize that many times the line between texts based on written words and those based on visual images is blurred. We see the value in being literate in the broadest sense—being able to make sense and respond to both visual and written symbols. Likewise, we also see the possibility of connecting visual texts and written texts to enhance the meaning of both.

In most reading programs, the texts that are used in classrooms are often quite limited. This is especially true with commercial reading programs. Texts used in reading instruction are still dominated by basal reading materials—a central anthology supplemented with additional materials. While use of anthologies has eroded a bit in the past few years, it is still estimated that 80 percent of classroom teachers rely on a basal reader for their reading programs (Gambrell 1992). This textbook approach to reading instruction is often mirrored with the use of additional textbooks in content areas—science, social studies, math, and language arts. Anyone familiar with current textbooks knows that they often contain a variety of texts within—poems, narrative stories, informational pieces, real-life applications—but the bottom line is that textbooks are the primary texts used in classrooms.

Two recent trends have expanded the texts that are used in classroom reading programs. The popularity of literature-based reading programs created a need for the use of real books in the classroom—trade books, not excerpts within anthologies, but *the real books* themselves. Readers' workshop, literature circles, book clubs, and other organizational formats increased the presence of trade books in many classrooms and actually supplanted the basal reader in some. In fact, core basal reading programs now often package trade books with their anthologies, which is easy to do since most publishers produce both instructional materials and trade books.

More recently, the reconceptualization of small-group reading instruction as guided reading has increased the presence of sets of leveled readers. These are often small books deliberately created for instructional use at differentiated levels of reading instruction. While these materials are separate books, they are not usually available as trade books for public consumption. As with trade books, publishers of many basal reading programs now package leveled readers or guided reading materials with their core reading programs.

We aim to present many different texts that will help you better meet the needs of the many different readers in your own classroom. To that end, we focus on texts that are undervalued and/or underutilized in classroom settings. We go beyond the basals and supplemental texts that dominate many classrooms. Our goal is to help you understand that if you expand the list of valued texts, you and your students will see *reading* as something more than just *reading books*.

Six Best Reasons for Using Many Texts with Many Readers

Why are we so intent on using many different texts within any given classroom? The following are our top six reasons.

Reason One: To Better Motivate All Children to Be Readers

The person who does not read has no advantage over the person who can not read.

—Mark Twain

Like Paris and Carpenter (2004), we believe that there are several factors that motivate readers. These include how readers perceive their abilities to read, the text, the reason for reading, and the surrounding environment. Take, for example, children who attend a sleepover and are told to bring their favorite book for reading and sharing with others. Children who elect to attend the event are sure to be motivated to read. After all, they get to choose the text with the purpose in mind. Self-selection means that they are likely to choose a text they feel they can read with ease. They need not be embarrassed when they share a part of it aloud with a friend. Likewise, because everyone will be reading, the environment will encourage all children to do the same. The person who chooses not to follow suit will be the odd one out and is likely to feel uncomfortable.

Teachers and children cause us to list motivation as the number one reason for using many texts with many readers. When asked about their number one concern in reading programs, teachers often identify motivation more than any other issue. Teachers ask, "What if they don't want to?" as much as "What if they can't?" Teachers are frustrated by the number of children who can read but never do. They are increasingly concerned that failing to address affective issues may be interfering with developing *readers*—students who will read long after they leave their school buildings.

But what about the children? What, if anything, do they have to say that might help teachers grapple with their reading motivation concerns? Acknowledging that motivation is multidimensional, Baker and Wigfield (1999) took a close look at what might motivate children to read to help address these most important questions. They actually went right to the source, the students themselves, to better understand what might motivate them to read. Baker and Wigfield developed an assessment tool that measured students in eleven key dimensions of motivation: self-efficacy, challenge, curiosity, enjoyment, importance, recognition, grades, competition, social interaction, compliance, and work avoidance. Their findings are telling. In short, they identified at least seven motivational profiles of readers. In Figure 1.1, we show profiles based in part on this research. We also describe each and offer some implications for matching readers and texts. We show which chapters in this book might be the starting points for developing

Figure 1.1 *Reader Profiles*

Profile	Description	Implications for Instruction	Best Chapters to Get Started
1: "I hate reading!"	Students who hate reading and will do anything to avoid it. They no longer see themselves as readers.	Create a display of many different text types and note if they are drawn to any of them. This might also help them establish their reading interests.	Real-Life Texts Cyber Texts Humorous Texts Multilevel Texts
2: "I don't like reading!"	Differing only in their intensity from group one, these students dislike reading and will do almost anything to avoid it. They, too, no longer see themselves as readers and see little value for the reading instruction that might help them.	As with the previous group, create a display of texts and observe students as they peruse them. They may gravitate toward texts that look the least like those used in school reading programs. Again, this may help them establish their reading interests.	Humorous Texts Real-Life Texts Magazines Newspapers Multilevel Texts
3: "I'm not very good at reading."	These are students who have little or no confidence in their reading ability.	The key for these students is finding any text that they can read. Short texts like articles and poems may be a good starting point. They can have success with these quickly and repeatedly. Once they are comfortable with these short texts, look for longer texts to stretch students so they see themselves as competent, comfortable, and confident readers. Series books may help the transition into becoming stronger, more confident readers.	Poetry Texts Magazines Newspapers Series Texts Multilevel Texts
4: "Reading is not very important to me."	These students do not struggle with reading but see reading as a low priority. They would rather be doing other activities. They often score high on the social dimension of motivation. They like to interact with others.	Consider texts that bring friends and books together. Plays and dramas inherently lend themselves to collective effort either in reading them or performing them in one of several ways (e.g., literature circles, choral reading, readers' theater).	Dramatic Texts Poetry Texts Series Texts Multilevel Texts

Figure 1.1 *Continued*

Profile	Description	Implications for Instruction	Best Chapters to Get Started
5: "I like reading competitions if I can win."	These students are often motivated by competition but only if they know they have a chance to win. If not, the motivation disappears quickly.	Just about any text can be used so long as there is a competition component. Some commercial competitive programs may be used to externally motivate these students. It may be most helpful if the program is used to help foster individual goal setting and to chart personal progress without a lot of outside comparisons. Some of these may be available online.	Cyber Texts Anthologies Series Texts
6: "My teacher says reading is important."	These students don't cause much trouble because they are often willing to do whatever teachers ask of them. They read because teachers have convinced them it is important.	Students who operate in a compliant mode will read almost anything we ask them to read, from selections in a traditional anthology to texts in cyberspace. They need to find what *they* want to read to become voracious readers.	Humorous Texts Series Texts Real-Life Texts
7: "I love reading."	These are the students who love to read and choose to read beyond the school walls.	These readers have already taken control of their reading habits. However, we want to build in access to all text types to ensure a well-rounded diet and encourage intertextual connections.	Newspapers Cyber Texts Real-Life Texts Magazines

(Based on Baker and Wigfield 1999)

instructional and motivational support for each type of profile. We also intend for this figure to make clear that like any aspect of reading instruction, motivation varies across readers, materials, and contexts. Expecting a one-size-fits-all solution to motivation denies the complexity of this issue. Educators need to look at a variety of ways to motivate students to become *readers*—students who not just can, but do, read.

More recently, Edmunds and Bauserman (2006) also reported that children are insightful about their own learning and can inform instruction. As a result of talking with ninety-one fourth-grade students, the researchers reported six categories that motivate children to read. For each category,

Category	Factors
1. Narrative text	1. Personal interests 2. Book characteristics 3. Choice
2. Expository text	1. Knowledge they gain from reading 2. Choice 3. Personal interest
3. Reading in general	1. Book characteristics 2. Knowledge they gain from reading
4. Sources of motivation	1. Family 2. Teachers 3. Themselves
5. Actions of others	1. Buying or giving books 2. Reading aloud to children 3. Sharing books
6. Book referral sources	1. School library 2. Teachers 3. Family members

(Based on Edmunds and Bauserman 2006)

Edmunds and Bauserman also showed the three motivating factors children mentioned most often. We show the categories and factors in Figure 1.2.

To help teachers interpret the results, Edmunds and Bauserman listed five recommendations to motivate students, all of which we draw on in this book: self-selection, attention to characteristics of books, which we expand to include other printed texts, personal interests, access to books, and active involvement with others.

Reason Two: To Shed Light on the Complexity of Reading

*While you can explain complex things simply, doing so does not change the
underlying complexity of the thing in the first place.*   —Jerry Harste

As we saw in the discussion of motivation, things are never quite as simple as they seem. This complexity is intensified when we realize that motivation is just one reader factor that contributes to successful reading. In addition to other reader factors, there are also a number of text factors and context

Figure 1.3 *An Interactive Model of Reading*

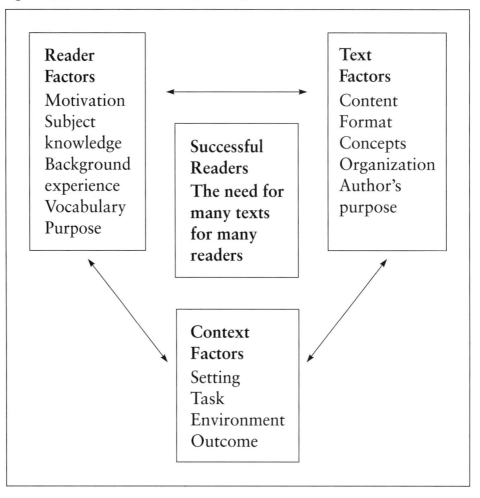

factors that can affect whether readers have success or not. Figure 1.3 shows the potential complexity of the interaction of all of these factors.

In their book *Authentic Literacy Assessment,* Lauren Leslie and Mary Jett-Simpson (1997) present a comprehensive look at the many factors that impact the interaction of readers, texts, and contexts. Their explanation helps clarify the interactive model of reading. Perhaps the main reason we need to remember this complexity is that it helps us better understand the children we teach. All too often, children are seen as the problem. Teachers lament that they're not motivated to read and provide a variety of reasons to explain why: too much television, too much time on the computer, too short of an attention span, and the list goes on. While there may be some truth to all of these reasons, when we consider an interactive model of reading, we realize that sometimes the blame does not rest entirely with the reader; the text itself can impact motivation and ultimate success as well as the context in which the reading is taking place, as Leslie and Jett-Simpson's explanation makes clear.

How Reader Factors Impact Texts

Prior knowledge: A reader who has knowledge of the subject of a text may have more success with that text than a reader who does not. Clearly we can all find all difficulties of texts at the same level—one which would be easy to read because the reader brings prior knowledge to the page and another that would be hard to read because the reader lacks that prior knowledge. With readers with many different backgrounds in the same class, we need to be prepared with texts that focus on many different subjects. Even when students are reading about the same subject, teachers may need to provide different texts to accommodate students with a low, moderate, or high knowledge of the subject.

Background experience: We need to consider a reader's background beyond her knowledge of the subject she's reading. Leslie and Jett-Simpson remind us that background experience also includes experience with the strategies needed to comprehend the text, text factors specific to the text, life experiences and emotions of the characters or people within the text, and reading patterns needed for adjusting to the difficulty of the text. Once again because the diverse group of readers in a classroom might vary on any or all of these aspects of reading, we need to be prepared with a variety of texts to better match the background experiences of readers.

Vocabulary: A specific aspect of background experience that may impact interactions with texts is the reader's vocabulary. A student may bring background knowledge to the page, but the level of sophistication at which the subject is being conceptually presented may limit his understanding. This sophistication often includes critical, specific vocabulary. Students may have different levels of knowledge of the concepts and the terminology being used. Texts need to be selected accordingly.

Purpose: Another factor that impacts the reader's interaction with the text is how the reader perceives the purpose for reading. If the teacher sets that purpose, the student must understand what that purpose is and how to achieve it. The reader must also see the teacher's purpose as meaningful and valuable. If the teacher does not set the purpose, readers must be able to focus on an appropriate purpose in approaching the text. Readers must also have the strategies needed to achieve that purpose and a belief that the outcome is valuable. Exposure to many texts contributes to learning about the many purposes for reading and becoming more strategic about adjusting behaviors based on those purposes.

How Contexts Impact Texts and Readers

Setting: In a balanced reading program, students will have time in which they read by themselves, with a partner, in a small group, and with the whole class. Each of these grouping formats has different outcomes for readers, all of which may be valuable for the students to experience. Text selection should be influenced by whether the student is reading alone or with others. Text selection should also be influenced by whether the student is reading in a large group or a small group. Clearly a text that might not be accessible in one setting might be in another, especially since the degree of teacher and peer support differs in each of these settings. Creating access to many texts better enables us to meet the goals of these different settings for reading.

Task: On the road to becoming an independent strategic reader, the student should be engaged in a variety of tasks within the classroom reading program. Sometimes those tasks are written. Sometimes they are oral. Sometimes the student answers questions. Sometimes she generates questions. Students are asked to respond by engaging in discussions with others. Students are also asked to respond through individual response projects. The task that the student is asked to complete can affect her interaction with the text. Certain texts lend themselves to certain tasks and using many texts provides the possibility of engaging students in a wider variety of tasks. Likewise, certain tasks can be accomplished best by creating specific texts. Students who are able to create a wider variety of texts will have more ways to respond to the texts they are reading.

Environment: Physical, sociological, and psychological factors all contribute to the environment in which reading takes place. Physically, the way the classroom is laid out, from adequate lighting to noise reduction, from ventilation to comfortable furniture, can make the reading interactions positive or negative. Sociologically, group compositions and interactions become critical. Has the teacher created a climate in which all voices are heard and honored? What are the stakes within the peer structures and culture? Teacher expectations and actions can contribute to a classroom atmosphere in which it is safe to take risks. Different expectations and actions may create a climate in which the stakes for taking risks are too high. It is important to remember that the environment can contribute to students seeing themselves as readers and writers and fostering a sense of community in which being a reader and writer is valued and allowed to flourish. These environments also are usually places in which many different texts, such as those we propose in this book, are used and valued.

Outcome: Would you interact differently with a text if you knew you were going to be graded on your response? What if you were going to be tested? What if that test result will become the basis for a critical decision about you as a reader? The use of the reading activity (perceived or otherwise) can certainly impact the interaction between readers and texts. We need to exercise caution in using specific kinds of texts for certain outcomes. If some types of texts are co-opted to meet external accountability demands, that may influence how students see them and use them in the future. By introducing a wider variety of texts in the classroom, we guard against the perception that reading is something you just do for tests or for schoolwork.

Reason Three: To Expand Children's Understandings of the Variety of Text Genres and Structures

> *Neither high-quality trade books nor practice books can serve as the sole diet of books for young readers to become proficient in literacy activities.*
>
> —P. David Pearson and Taffy Raphael

> *Children read to learn—even when they are reading fantasy, nonsense, light verse, comics, or the copy on cereal packets, they are expanding their minds all the time, enlarging their vocabulary, making discoveries; it is all new to them.*
>
> —Joan Aiken

We can see that a variety of both reading factors and context factors creates a need for using a variety of texts in classroom reading programs. But when we also add text factors to that equation, we have just intensified the complexity of what it takes to read successfully. Text factors can often contribute to making a text more or less considerate for the reader. Considerate text is often more reader-friendly; students often find it easier to understand and learn from text that is considerate (Armbruster 1984). Let's begin by looking at two critical text factors: genres and text structures. We'll then consider four additional text factors: format, content, concepts, and author's purpose.

Genres

Genre is traditionally defined as "a category used to classify literary works usually by form, technique or content" (Harris and Hodges 1995, 94). But as *genre* is reconceptualized to include aspects of the communicative act beyond textual features, the focus and application of *genre* is altered and its definition becomes more elusive. Lattimer observes that "genres are proliferating like snowflakes in a blizzard" (2003, x). She points out that new print technologies are creating new genres ranging from text messages to interactive role-playing games. In fact, one relatively new genre is multigenre (Danielson and Harrington 2005; Laminack and Bell 2004). As the term indicates, authors employ more than one genre to write a meaningful story. *Every Man for Himself: Ten Short Stories About Being a Guy* (Mercado 2005) and *Moondog* (Rowe 2005) are but two examples of multigenre texts. Yet another example is *Criss Cross,* the 2005 Newbery Award–winning novel by Lynn Rae Perkins that intersperses lyrics, poems, plays, music, drawings, and photographs in telling its story of a group of friends.

In this book, we primarily focus on a more classic view of genre and use it to help us classify types of texts that share certain features and distinguish them from other types of texts. Some genres define narrative texts and some define informational texts. Some can actually define both fiction and nonfiction texts. Buss and Karnowski (2000) use four broad categories to define common genres that share a narrative story structure: fiction (including realistic fiction and mysteries), traditional literature (fables, folktales), fantasy (including modern folktales), and nonfiction (especially biographies). These genres all share a structure that basically includes a definable story line (beginning, middle, and end) and has elements like setting, characters, goals, conflicts, attempts to solve the conflict, and resolutions. Buss and Karnowski (2002) also identify six genres that are not structured with narrative story lines and tend to define forms of nonfiction: recounts and procedural, sequentially ordered, informational, journalistic, and persuasive texts (see Figure 1.4).

Why is this discussion of genres important? Being able to recognize genres becomes a useful instructional instrument. Buss and Karnowski (2002) argue that in the past, literature study was primarily divided into two categories: fiction and nonfiction. Those categories, however, end up being "too broad to reflect adequately the richness and the variations within each genre of text" (3). They suggest teaching genres beyond just fiction and nonfiction. Harris and Hodges (1995) point out that even very young children get very adept at identifying familiar genres like fairytales and mysteries after being exposed to them. Once students can identify a genre, they can adjust their reading and response strategies to more adequately handle the texts in front of them. Lattimer (2003) says that genre is the first frame for the reader's prediction. It eliminates potential distractions and makes reading easier. She concludes: "If we figure out that this is a poem, we'll be expecting the

Figure 1.4 *Genres and Instructional Texts*

Genre	Text Implications	Appropriate Chapter(s)
Realistic fiction	Stories that could happen in the real world, in a time and setting that are possible and characters that are true to life	Series Texts Dramatic Texts Anthologies Multilevel Texts
Mystery	Realistic fiction characterized by scare factor, suspense, and quickly paced action; promotes active participation of the reader to make sense of the clues provided	Series Texts Dramatic Texts
Traditional fable and folktale	Body of ancient stories and poems that grew out of the human quest to understand the natural and spiritual world, passed down by people who told stories	Poetry Texts Anthologies
Fantasy	Literature in which the events, settings, or characters are outside the realm of possibility but become convincingly real	Series Texts Humorous Texts Multilevel Texts
Modern folktale	A blending of modern fantasy and traditional folktale; usually a modern tale using the story line from an old folktale	Humorous Texts
Biography	An account of a person's life written by someone else, combining elements of expository writing (information from the person's life) with narrative writing (an entertaining account the reader can relate to)	Magazines Newspapers Multilevel Texts
Recount	Written to retell events, with purpose of either informing or entertaining or both	Newspapers Magazines Cyber Texts
Procedural	Written to help readers follow a set of steps to achieve an intended purpose	Real-Life Texts Magazines Newspapers
Sequentially ordered	Uses a predetermined pattern to present information sequentially	Multilevel Texts Real-Life Texts Magazines
Informational	Nonfiction writing that has the main purpose of presenting factual information on a specific topic or event	Real-Life Texts Magazines Newspapers Multilevel Texts
Journalistic	Text divided into different sections to cover interrelated topics including reoccurring features with a variety of purposes	Magazines Newspapers Cyber Texts
Persuasive	Presents an argument or an opinion in an attempt to convince the reader to accept the writer's point of view	Newspapers Real-Life Texts Cyber Texts

(Based on Buss and Karnowski 2000)

language to do different things than if it were a set of mechanical instructions. We'll read it differently" (x). Buss and Karnowski (2002) also remind us that when students can identify the elements of the genres they are reading, they will be better able to create those genres when they are writing.

Text Structures

One of the features genres usually share is an internal organization. The texts within a genre are often structured in a certain way. Structures vary within and across categories of texts. The ability of readers to recognize those structures provides another frame to assist in reading and responding to the text. As with knowing the genre, knowing the text structure also narrows the possibilities and eliminates the distractions. The value in knowing about these different structures is that it better ensures successful reading experiences with a wide variety of texts. In other words, the more texts the reader encounters through deliberate, planned instruction designed to provide exposure to many different texts, the more structures the reader becomes familiar with. The more structures the reader is familiar with, the greater his potential success with handling a variety of texts.

Unfortunately, the steady diet of narrative stories that feeds the instructional menu of young readers often narrowly defines the types of structures with which many children become familiar (Duke 2000). It begins to define the type of text with which they will have success. We see this in the most recent international comparison of fourth-grade readers (Mullis, Martin, Gonzalez, and Kennedy 2003). U.S. students were among the best narrative story readers in the world. Only Swedish students were significantly higher than U.S. students on the narrative scale measure used in the test. U.S. students, however, were less strong on the expository scale measure. This reflects a lesser ability to handle informational texts. Some researchers would argue that this finding shouldn't be surprising since the instructional program of elementary school often contains an abundance of narrative texts and very few expository texts. Duke (2000) found that students in classrooms she observed spent on average only 3.6 minutes with informational text per day. Hall, Sabey, and McClellan (2005) feel that this neglect of expository text in the primary grades may actually contribute to the decline in reading achievement after third grade often referred to as the fourth-grade slump.

While some skills and strategies transcend different texts, others are specific to certain texts. This is especially true with text structures. It's hard for children to learn how to read and write texts with many different structures if they are being taught using only one type of text. Sometimes this imbalance shows itself in popular classroom routines. For example, reading aloud to students almost always involves stories. One way to address this concern is to read aloud texts with structures other than narrative story lines. With this type of instructional attention, children begin to develop an ear for how different texts are written. Exposure is essential. We know if we help students hear and see all types of texts over time, we plant the structures in their heads, which makes it easier for them to read and create texts with the same structures. In Figure 1.5, we illustrate different text structures and the best instructional texts to use to help readers understand and use those structures. A visit to either http://freeology.com/graphicorgs/index.php or www.teachnology.com/worksheets/graphic will yield a wealth of graphic organizers designed for each structure. The blank forms are free.

Wiliams (2005) points out that informational text is generally more difficult to comprehend because of the variety of structures and unfamiliar content. Several researchers suggest that one main reason for this difficulty is that students can't see the basic structure of the texts they are reading, but if students develop a good understanding of these structures, they will have fewer comprehension difficulties (Dymock 2005). Other researchers suggest that if teachers explicitly and systematically teach text structures, comprehension increases (Sweet and Snow 2003; Duke 2000). To more easily and effectively teach about text structures, we recommend using a variety of texts with a variety of structures. For example, using a think-aloud, we can point out the author's use of signal words. We can also explain that every author uses a blueprint to write and that these blueprints change depending on the author's purpose for writing the text. We can then make the structure more transparent by showing students the specific structure via an appropriate graphic organizer.

Other Text Factors

In addition to text structures and genres, there are four other text factors we need to highlight: format, content, concepts, and author's purpose.

Format: Experts have used the terms *considerate* and *inconsiderate* to describe the way texts are designed (Kantor, Anderson, and Armbruster 1983). A user-friendly text may facilitate understanding. A clean arrangement, clear headings, strategic introductions and summaries, and graphic aids may all assist students in their learning. Format issues also include being able to recognize and deal with different types of books (picture books versus chapter books) and genres (informational texts versus poetry). (Note: For a good discussion of factors that contribute to making texts considerate, go to www .glencoe.com/sec/teachingtoday/subject/considerate_text.phtml.)

Figure 1.5 *Text Structures and Instructional Materials*

Text Structure	Description	Example	Signal Words	Questions to Consider
Description/ list structure	This structure resembles an outline. Each section opens with its main idea and then elaborates on it, sometimes dividing the elaboration into subsections.	A book may tell all about whales or describe what the geography is like in a particular region.	*for example, for instance, specifically, in particular, in addition*	What are you describing? What are its qualities?
Cause-and-effect structure	In texts that follow this structure, the reader is told the result of an event or occurrence and the reasons it happened.	A text about weather could describe patterns that explain why a big snowstorm occurred.	*consequently, therefore, as a result, thereby, leads to*	What are the causes and effects of this event? What might happen next?
Comparison-contrast structure	Texts that follow this structure tell about the differences and similarities of two or more objects, places, events, or ideas by grouping their traits for comparison.	A book about ancient Greece may explain how the Spartan women were different from the Athenian women.	*however, unlike, like, by contrast, yet, in comparison, although, whereas, similar to, different from*	What are the similar and different qualities of these things? What qualities of each thing correspond to one another? In what way?
Order/ sequence structure	Texts that follow this structure tell the order in which steps in a process or series of events occur.	A book about the American Revolution might list the events leading to the war. Another book might tell the steps involved in harvesting blue crabs.	*next, first, last, second, another, then, additionally*	What happened? What is the sequence of events? What are the substages?

Figure 1.5 *Continued*

Text Structure	Graphic Organizer(s)	Best Texts
Description/list structure	Bubble Map 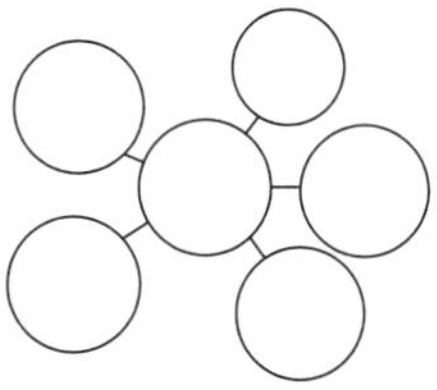	Magazines Newspapers
Cause-and-effect structure	Multiple Causes Map 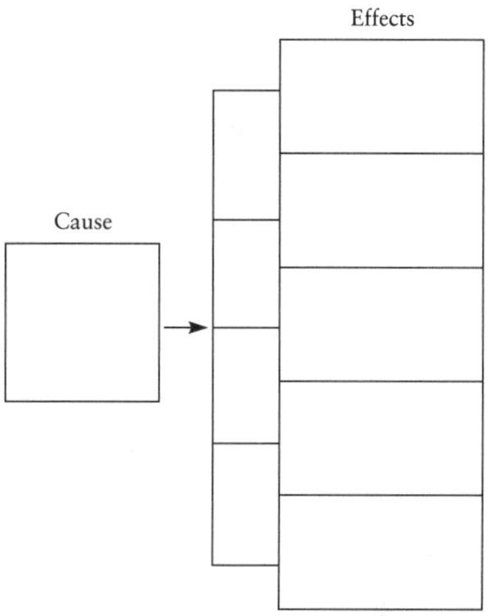 Multiple Effects Map 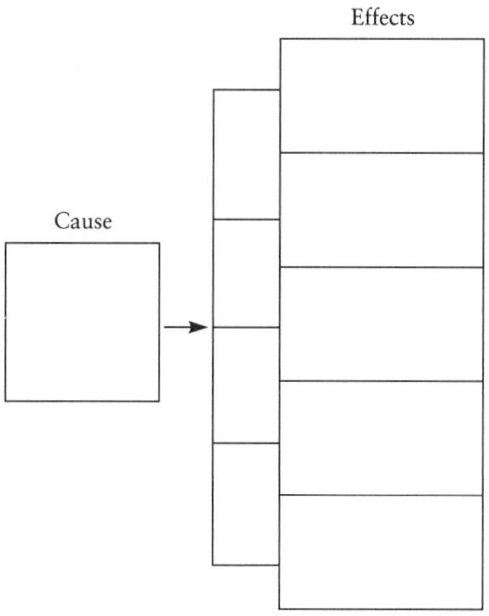	Mysteries Magazines Newspapers

Continues

Figure 1.5 *Continued*

Text Structure	Graphic Organizer(s)	Best Texts
Comparison-contrast structure	Ladder Map Compare and Contrast Modified Venn	Multilevel Texts
Order/sequence structure	Time Line Flowchart	Real-Life Texts

(Based on "Text Structures," from the Florida Online Reading Professional Development website, created by Central Florida University College of Education for Just Read, Florida! [www.itrc.ucf.edu/forpd/strategies/default.html])

Content: Leslie and Jett-Simpson (1997) note that content is shaped by the topic being covered in the text as well as the depth of that coverage. What is covered and how much it is covered can influence the interaction between reader and text. And let's remember that narrative stories feature content, too. Certain literary elements, story characteristics, or themes can either contribute to or impede readers' meaning making.

Concepts: The concepts within a text may appear in different ways, and some presentations make texts difficult to read. For example, readers may encounter a dense text with many different ideas imbedded in the text, and concepts and technical vocabulary that are not well defined, creating complexity that might make it harder to understand the text. A less dense presentation written in clear, basic prose will probably make the text easier to read.

Author's purpose: Does the author's purpose impact the interaction between the text and the reader? Consider if the author's purpose is to primarily entertain the reader. How might the interaction be different if the author's primary purpose was to inform or influence the reader? Each of these purposes makes the interaction easier or harder, depending on the reader. We've all witnessed what can happen when readers literally interpret a text intended as satire. Exposing students to texts that have different author purposes, then, fosters a more critical evaluation of texts by readers.

Reason Four: To Make More Texts Acceptable and Accessible in and out of School

Bad breath is better than no breath. —Dav Pilkey

*There is nothing necessarily beneficial about a habit.
Television can be a habit. Cocaine can be a habit. Reading,
too, can be a habit. The question is: What sort of habit?* —Tom Engelhardt

When we talk about creating a reading habit in students, there's always an interesting tension between the "at least they're reading" folks and the "I can't believe what they're reading" folks. How do you get the reading habit started, and how do you keep it moving in an increasingly more positive direction? We believe allowing the use of many different texts in the classroom is the answer to both questions. Unfortunately in this debate, sometimes texts used in school are seen as quality literature and what children read outside of school is considered anything but. A "good" book can and often is defined in one of two ways: quality in terms of literary traits, and taste.

Figure 1.6 *Classifying Texts on Merit and Response*

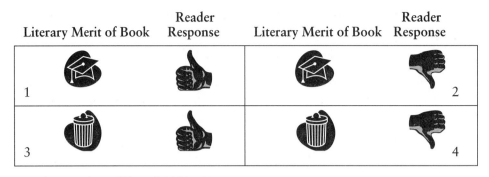

(Based on Jacobs and Tunnell 2004, 18)

Usually when we talk of a book being good, we are referring to taste rather than literary elements. Jacobs and Tunnell (2004) point out that considering reader response (i.e., taste) and literary merit sets up potential disconnects between the two (see Figure 1.6).

In quadrant 1 of the table in Figure 1.6, the literary merit of the book is deemed good, and the reader response is positive. In quadrant 2, the literary merit is deemed good but the reader response is negative. In quadrant 3, the literary merit is deemed poor, but the reader likes the text. In quadrant 4, the literary merit is deemed poor and the reader does not like the text.

While it might be easy to agree that any text with both literary merit and positive response deserves a place in a classroom reading program (quadrant 1) and any text without literary merit or positive response probably does not (quadrant 4), we must remember that both literary merit and reader response are aggregated across reviewers and readers and might not be shared by all. Perhaps more importantly, even when literary merit is agreed upon as the critical factor in defining what texts are acceptable and accessible in the classroom, considering literary merit alone sets up a potential problem for teachers trying to meet the needs of diverse learners. Since literary merit and reader response are determined by two very different groups of readers, many texts judged to have literary merit will not draw a desirable response from readers (quadrant 2). Many texts that have a positive reader response won't be judged to have literary quality (quadrant 3). If a large number of texts that are enjoyed by children are automatically eliminated from the classroom reading program, we limit our ability to draw from a variety of texts to reach readers even when one of those texts might be the best match for helping a child.

If children are already engaged in reading quadrant 3 texts, why not capitalize on that to advance the goals of the school reading program? If we value texts in quadrant 3 within classroom reading programs, the end result is likely to be that more texts in quadrant 2 become more accessible and acceptable. Paris and Carpenter note, "Children who are successful, enthusiastic readers outside school, but not inside, are less at risk than children who read only in school under duress but not independently" (2004, 72). If quadrant 3 texts are used to help children become increasingly more competent, confident, and comfortable readers, the students may grow in their abilities to respond more positively to an increasing number of texts judged to have literary merit.

Beyond creating a broader definition of good books, though, another reason for using many texts with many readers focuses on the issues of acceptability and accessibility. As Roller and Fielding (1992) observed, there comes a time in some reading programs in which the texts seen as acceptable for use in the classroom are no longer accessible for some of the students in that classroom. On the other hand, texts that would be accessible for some students in that classroom are no longer seen as acceptable. Take, for example, an intermediate-grade classroom in which the primary text for reading instruction is a sophisticated novel with a reading level beyond some of the students in that class. Those students would be better matched with a short chapter book by the same author. Unfortunately, the chapter book is perceived as a baby book and carries a stigma in this classroom. Suddenly what is acceptable is now no longer accessible for some, and what is accessible for some is no longer acceptable. With a broader view of texts and a more frequent use of a variety of texts, we are better able to make sure that all texts are acceptable in the classroom, especially those that might be accessible for the students who have the greatest need for practice and support.

Remember the often told story about a teacher saying to a distracted student, "Put down that book and come back to the reading table!" We all can tell stories about how suppressing literacy initiatives in school by making tasks and texts unacceptable or inaccessible often led to the activities emerging outside the school walls. Michael Opitz tells the story of how his son and three of his friends actually dropped their journalism class during school and then spent hours outside of school creating their own newspapers and swapping them with one another online. Matthew Zbaracki's brother did the same and created an underground newspaper. Michael Ford (2004) wondered if the school co-opted out-of-school literate activities for school literacy programs, would children find them less desirable and return to reading books as a way to maintain their "subversive" activities. The message seems clear: if we want children to regard what they learn in school as connected to their real life outside of school, we need to fill classroom reading programs with a wide range of real texts.

Reason Five: To Help Children Develop an Understanding of Intertexuality

I began with the shared book The Girl Who Loved Wild Horses. *. . . Then we read* Hawk I'm Your Brother. *. . . We learned something about Native American culture. We compared and contrasted these two stories. This led us to a book brought in by a child called* Where the Buffaloes Begin *. . . which led us to studying the bison and its habitat and adaptations. This led us to the Native American relationship to the bison and the near extinction of the bison by the white hunters, as well as change in the habitat with the westward movement of the European settlers. This led us to reading a biography of Sitting Bull and learning of the Sioux Indian struggle for survival. . . . We got involved in real life dreams and excitement. We learned about heroes who would not trade for easier wishes—Rudy Sato in* Hawk I'm Your Brother *wanted to fly and he wouldn't trade for easier wishes—neither would Sitting Bull, neither would General Custer and now we're reading about Martin Luther King who also wouldn't trade for easier wishes.*
—Nancy Decker

All of the "texts" in our world are constructed with messages. One way to broaden students' ability to interpret text and recognize what is embedded in messages is to make connections across texts.
—Janice Strop, Holly Dionne, and Richard Kuhnen

As the students in Nancy Decker's classroom discovered, to study complex subjects and explore important themes, the use of a single text would be somewhat limiting in its ability to convey all aspects and nuances of that subject. Strop (2005) began considering this as she prepared a thematic unit on child labor. Instead of starting with a single text, she developed a text set that included the texts of "our world"—books, ads, magazines, music, websites, films, and TV shows. By using a text set as the heart of her instruction, she was able to provide her students an opportunity to respond to a variety of perspectives across a range of difficulty levels, work with a variety of text structures and purposes, and engage in diverse thinking about those ideas. Working with her colleague Linda Gordy, she developed a social studies unit focused on child labor practices. They began to see that their use of an excerpt titled "Breaker Boys" from Susan Bartoletti's book *Growing Up in Coal Country* (1999) was enhanced when it was supplemented by the use of other texts and media. What was hard to visualize in the book suddenly became more apparent when the students were invited to read historical photographs from the same time period of Bartoletti's book. Strop and Gordy provided access to five additional texts that explored child labor themes, both narrative (Katherine Paterson's *Lyddie* [1992]) and informational (Russell Freeman's *Kids at Work* [1998]). Using a RAFT activity (role, audience, form, and topic—with these four points in mind, we can create a meaningful context for students' writing) to respond to the texts, students explored even more formats, including drafting a petition for the U.S. Congress to regulate child labor.

As readers try to make sense of and critically respond to what they have read, they need to make connections. Keene and Zimmermann (1997) identify three primary types of connections: text to self, text to world, and text to text. The latter category is often labeled intertextuality. What Strop and Gordy (2003) are intentionally doing is fostering intertextuality as they move toward their instructional goals for their students. Schole (1985) defines intertextuality as reading both across and against texts. If every text stands alone as an experience, the potential for critical dialogue and more sophisticated understandings is very limited. Consider fractured fairly tales like *The True Story of the Three Little Pigs* (Scieszka 1996) and *The Frog Prince: Continued* (Scieszka 1994). While the texts could be enjoyed on their own, understanding and potential for response grows if one is able to bring knowledge of the original fairy tales to the books as they are read. It is making connections to our experience, what we know about the world and what we have read in other texts, that allows students to move to higher levels of comprehension.

Reason Six: To Address the Oversimplification of Leveling Systems Often Used to Determine Which Books Children Should Read

> *We seem to be in the midst of leveling mania in which massive amount of time, money, and energy are devoted to organizing books by reading levels. . . . It appears that teachers are driven to attach a level to every text that students encounter during their school day.* —Brenda Dzaldo and Shelley Peterson

> *Fitting people with books is about as difficult as fitting them with shoes.* —Sylvia Beach

The previous reasons clearly present a growing rationale for using different kinds of texts in classroom reading programs that contain many different kinds of readers. Let's add one more reason: our concerns with the growing use of leveling schemes to classify readers and texts. We are concerned that these schemes have in one way oversimplified the complexity of the interaction between readers and their texts that we previously discussed (see page 8) while at the same time adding an unnecessary complexity to the matching of readers and texts. First let's look at how leveling has simplified the complexity of reading. Of the reader, text, and context factors that we have discussed, most leveling schemes address only text factors. Even when they focus on text features, it is nearly impossible for leveling systems to accommodate all of the many different text features that need to be considered in determining the complexity of a text. In traditional readability measures, sentence length (number of words in a sentence) and word length (number of syllables in one hundred words) were privileged as the two components used to determine the level of the text. At least now, many more factors are considered. In one set of leveling criteria, twenty-five characteristics of five basic features were considered: book, text, illustration, language and sentence, and story. The problem is even the most sophisticated measure would not be able to incorporate all potential text features. Because of this, the systems fall short of capturing the true level of books. Furthermore, since no system takes into account any reader or context factors, the level may be even more questionable for any given reader in any given context.

Likewise, assessment systems that attempt to determine the level of the reader privilege certain aspects of the reading process. Traditional measures like informal reading inventories might focus on word accuracy, fluency, and/or comprehension. Each of these critical aspects of reading is further dependent on the actual tools and techniques defining the measurement. Word accuracy might actually mean reading words in a list on one measure and reading words in connected text on another measure. Again, while new assessment tools have become more sophisticated in trying to capture other aspects of the reader, no measure will capture the entire complexity of what the reader brings to the page.

Leveling systems that focus exclusively on the reader or on the text also draw attention away from the actual unique interactions between individual readers and individual texts. While such systems can help us provide better matches between students and books, there is nothing automatic about matching a certain-level student with a certain-level book. The interactions between readers and books may work in some cases and may not work in others, and the levels more often than not have little to do with it. Teachers have often seen students at a certain level have success with a book that was actually at a higher level. Teachers have also seen students at a certain level struggle with a book at the same or a lower level. This again demonstrates that there are other factors at work in completing a successful transaction between the reader and the text.

One obvious factor ignored by most leveling systems is that the interaction between the reader and the text always takes place in a context. As we've discussed, certain contexts can facilitate interactions between readers and texts. Other contexts impede interactions between readers and texts. Everything from the physical dimensions to the emotional feel of these contexts plays a role in shaping the interaction. In each of these cases, leveling is not the only or even the most important factor that needs to be considered in matching texts and readers. These contexts may be defined by the school culture in which they take place, but they may also be shaped by broader sociocultural factors that transcend the school environment (Kucer 2005). This sociocultural aspect of the reading process is nearly impossible to capture in leveling systems, especially when those systems are marketed to national audiences regardless of the school cultures and sociocultural contexts in which they exist.

Now let's look at how these schemes complicate some simple concepts. Basically, the idea of matching readers and texts makes sense. Readers should be able to read or at least work on texts with which they are matched. It makes even more sense as a way to address a pervasive problem seen in many classrooms—many readers spending too much time with texts they can't read. But, again, implementing this idea in a classroom of diverse readers is complicated by these schemes. Leveling systems that create large numbers of discrete levels of readers and texts do so in a way that has to be a bit arbitrary and capricious. What truly distinguishes a level M book from a level N book? Is that difference meaningful enough to suggest an instructional implication? Imagine the frustration of teachers trying to juggle all their students at all these different levels when collapsed groups and combined levels might be more manageable and yield just as good results. Limiting a reader to texts classified at these discrete levels may actually prevent the teacher from providing a better match for the child.

Another problem with any leveling system is it privileges the texts it classifies and categorizes. Because certain leveling systems are mandated for use in classrooms, teachers and students may decide not to use a text because it has not been classified by the system (e.g., almost any text published since the last update of the leveling system). Even when a text is identified by a system, teachers and students may also decide not to select it because of the way it is classified by the system (e.g., points are too low, level is too high). Finally, because most leveling systems focus exclusively on trade books, other types of texts are marginalized because they are not even considered by the systems.

Finally, censorship is another major problem that those selling and/or using some leveling systems create. That is, children are given a test to determine their level. They then are required to choose books with a corresponding level (yes, some school personnel level their entire school libraries!) and, in so doing, get credit or points that add up to a total score that is externally rewarded. If students want to read a book beneath their level, they are most often permitted to do so, but they are given no credit toward the final prize. So books such as Lowry's *Number the Stars* (1990), which in our opinion is a valuable read for many children and adults, may not be read by children who are assigned a higher level. And if you think we are exaggerating, think again! This scenario is repeatedly reported to us as we work with teachers and parents across the United States and abroad. Consider a recent event a colleague of Michael Opitz's recently reported. She was in her son's school observing her son select a leveled book for his independent reading. Her son is considered to be a 4.2-level reader, so he must choose from the 4.2 books if he wants credit for reading. "Imagine," she stated, "having your second-grade son read Judy Blume's *Deenie* because it has a 4.2 level!"

As you can see, we need not travel to River City for troubles with leveling systems; we have them right here at home.

Many Readers, Many Texts

In their book *Read Anything Good Lately?* Susan Allen and Jane Lindaman (2003) alphabetically present a young girl reader reading twenty-six different texts in twenty-six different contexts. From an atlas at the airport through joke books in the Jacuzzi, from poetry on a park bench to the zodiac horoscope at the zoo, Allen and Lindaman capture the wide variety of texts that fill the daily literate lives of all of us. Why would we as teachers not want to capitalize on this? Conventional wisdom suggests that if a classroom is filled with many different readers, a teacher would want to use many different texts to meet the needs of those readers. But we seem to live in a time when one-size-fits-all solutions dominate our educational practices. In this chapter, we have provided six important reasons for expanding our view of acceptable texts for use in classroom reading programs. The use of a greater variety of texts helps address the

- complexity of motivating readers

- variation in reader factors and the contexts in which they read

- need for students to learn about a variety of text structures and genres

- accessibility and acceptability of classroom texts

- ability of learners to make intertextual connections

- problems with leveling systems

Grounded in this rationale and theoretical framework, we will next explain how you can use many different types of texts in your classroom reading program, including

- magazines

- poetry

- multilevel texts

- newspapers

- series texts

- humorous texts

- dramatic texts

- real-life texts

- anthologies

- cyber texts

Not sure where to begin? We suggest starting with those that might be the easiest to add to your program. We wrote each chapter as a stand-alone piece, so the chapters need not be read in any particular order. Every chapter follows the same format:

- a brief description

- six reasons for using the specific text

- suggestions for how to use the text for a variety of reading experiences (e.g., read-aloud, shared reading, guided reading, and independent reading)

- a scenario showing how to use the text with younger elementary-aged students

- a scenario showing how to use the text with older elementary-aged students

We also include sample titles, websites, and references.

Then continue to visit the chapters on other texts you may not have considered to get ideas on how to add them as well. Before you are finished, your view of texts and readers will shift. You will begin to see that you are surrounded by readers even when they don't have a book in their hands.

CHAPTER 2

Magazines

Few treasures brighten a child's eyes and smile, engage their curiosity, and sharpen their knowledge like a magazine full of color and dreams.

—http://childmagmonth.org

A Brief Description

Magazines: We all know what they are, or do we? When thinking about writing this brief description, Michael Opitz decided to consult the dictionary to check his understanding of the word we often utter without much regard to its descriptors. Much to his surprise, he discovered that Webster's offers up five distinct definitions for *magazine*. The fourth definition, "A periodical containing miscellaneous pieces (as articles, stories, poems) often illustrated," provides the basis for this chapter. Columns of text, pictures with short captions, brief statements related to many different topics, visual displays, and advertisements come together as editors create magazines focused on an array of topics ranging from animals to consumer reports to people. Like any good writers, magazine editors think about the intended audience to guide their content selection. And, as a perusal of the magazine section of a bookstore or grocery store shows, we are not at a loss for a variety of magazines (and these don't even include those stored behind the counter for the most discriminating buyer!).

Why Use Them?

In Chapter 1, we provided six reasons for using a variety of texts. Let's take a look at how these apply to magazines.

To Better Motivate All Readers

As mentioned in Chapter 1, motivation and interest go a long way toward engaging readers. Magazines are motivational for several reasons. First, they provide readers with current information that enables them to connect and expand their knowledge about recent events or celebrities. This type of information is often omitted from other texts because of the publishing process. Take the December 2005–January 2006 issue of *National Geographic Kids,* for example. One of the articles focuses on recovering from the recent South Asian tsunami. While this natural disaster is significant enough to include in future texts, the magazine seized the moment in this issue. And the dinosaur discovery revealed by scientists on October 13, 2005, as reported in the November 2005 issue of *Time for Kids,* is yet another example of a current event that will undoubtedly be included in future dinosaur books. Most textbooks take nearly one year to produce, however. Therefore, including the most current information such as these two examples here is next to impossible.

Second, several children's magazines include articles written by peers. As a result of reading these selections, students have opportunities to interact with others the same age, a motivating factor indeed. Reading these articles also helps students see that they, too, can be authors and what they have to say is of importance to an audience beyond their classmates.

Third, it seems as though most youngsters we teach have one major life mission: to be a grown-up. They see the types of texts that those older than themselves read and they, too, want to be part of that club. Fortunately, there are so many magazines at all age levels that children can enjoy their childhood years and appear as grown-ups simultaneously. *Time* and *National Geographic* are but two magazines that have a version for children with covers that are nearly identical to the adult versions. Length of the magazine and sophistication of the content are the two primary differences. So the entire family can read the same magazine, or so the cover would have us believe!

Fourth, as the second and third reader profiles in Chapter 1 illustrate (see page 5, Figure 1.1), some children find reading difficult and see little value in it. Because magazines include several different types of writing of varying lengths, using them with these students can be a way to change their attitude about themselves as readers. For example, instead of having to read an entire chapter or page, students can read captions of pictures on different pages. They can also read labels of diagrams. They can read the short sidebars that often appear next to full-length articles. They can read the word bubbles that are sometimes used to represent a talking character. While each of these reading experiences focuses on short pieces of text, taken together, they give students much practice with reading. While it may appear to the reader that little reading is happening, nothing could be further from the truth. That is, taken together, all of the parts contribute to a significant whole.

To Shed Light on the Complexity of Reading

Reading is a complex behavior (see Chapter 1). Learning how to negotiate different texts is one part of this complexity. Students need to understand that different texts are written with different structures if they are to best comprehend them. Magazines present their own unique structure. For example, they are compilations of many different kinds of writing, such as advertisements, labels, articles, picture captions, and poems. Because they are really more of a collection, they can be read in a nonlinear fashion. Likewise, reading the contents of the entire magazine is rarely necessary. Magazines, then, help round out students' understanding about how to read texts.

To Expand Children's Understandings of the Variety of Text Genres and Structures

All texts have their own structure, magazines included. Having an understanding of the structure helps readers negotiate the text and better comprehend it (Meyer and Rice 1984). To get the most out of reading magazines, students need to become "magazine literate" (Stoll 1997, vii). In other words, they need to know how the magazine is organized, where to locate information, the different types of writing (e.g., articles, advertisements, captions), and the format (e.g., columns). While some students may independently learn how magazines work, calling attention to the structure better ensures that all students gain an understanding of magazine structure.

To Make More Texts Acceptable and Accessible in and out of School

Children read a variety of texts when given the opportunity. But some children view themselves as nonreaders because they think of readers as those who read books. However, this is a serious misconception that magazines have the potential to counter. If children see that magazines are valued in school, as evidenced by how they are used and permitted, magazines provide another reading alternative.

But beyond this acceptance, magazines make text accessible for students who struggle with reading other types of texts. Magazines can serve as a scaffold, enabling children deemed below level to rise to the occasion. Here's why.

First, magazines have limited information. Instead of having to read long selections, students can read short snippets, making their success more likely.

Second, students need not read the entire magazine. They can be directed to read certain pieces and then share with others who read different pieces. With careful planning, which includes using what we know about our students, we can assign different sections to students that will enable their reading success. Some students might read short blurbs whereas others might read the diagrams. Still others can read the picture captions and some can read full-length articles. Students can then provide information to one another about their various readings, learning from their peers.

Finally, magazines can make reading more accessible to children outside of school. Some children have limited reading materials at home, and magazines can help fill this void. For example, a classroom magazine subscription such as *Time for Kids* yields one copy for each student. Students can take their individual copies home for further reading practice. And, as the International Reading Association Board of Directors notes in its position statement *Providing Books and Other Print Materials for Classroom and School Libraries* (1999), voluntary practice leads to better readers.

To Help Children Develop an Understanding of Intertextuality

Texts link to texts. This is one major idea we want to convey to children so that they can see how different references might be connected. It is a way of confirming and validating ideas. Magazines provide a useful service here. For example, students might first read something about a current natural disaster such as a recent hurricane. They then might read about natural disasters in other texts such as newspapers, cyber texts, or books. They can look for commonalities among all of these sources to determine just what makes a natural disaster. Articles often refer to other sources, like books and websites, for more information.

At the current time, it appears as though we are in a leveling frenzy. And as already discussed, there are many issues that need to be considered when thinking about leveling books and children. We need not concern ourselves with these issues when using age-appropriate magazines. We can take off the leveling label and, as noted earlier, scaffold the instruction so that all students can successfully engage with the magazine in one way or another.

How Might They Be Used?

Read-aloud: We often think about reading books aloud, but magazines are perfect for read-alouds as well. It might be that you want to share a current event that is reported in a magazine. You might want to point out how a diagram is used. At still other times, you might want to read aloud advertisements in magazines and have students listen for a specific purpose such as a propaganda technique or bias.

Shared reading: Some children's magazines such as *Time for Kids: The Big Picture* come with an enlarged version of the issue. Consequently, the issue can be used for whole-group shared reading because it is large enough for all students to see. Using the magazine in this way is an option when you want to teach the entire class something about the organization of the magazine and/or content in the magazine. The enlarged version gives all a common focal point, making the lesson more effective than one in which students have to follow along in their own copies.

Guided reading: Small-group guided reading is a perfect fit for magazines. Magazines can serve as the reading material when you want to teach children a specific skill. You might want to teach them about magazine features. Then again, you might want to use magazines to provide students with more general knowledge. Then, too, you might want to use them to broaden their knowledge base in terms of a specific content area. One of the luxuries of small-group guided reading, assuming that those children working away from the teacher are meaningfully engaged, is that you can provide students with help as needed.

Independent reading: Magazines are a sure fit with independent reading. Students can select from several titles and can read those parts that they find most meaningful. As they turn the pages and look at small snippets of text, they are increasing their vocabularies and are reading. And, as reading authorities such as Frank Smith (2004) and Stephen Krashen (2004) remind us, children learn to read by reading. They are engaged, which means that they are more apt to learn new content or add to their knowledge base.

Using Magazines with Younger Elementary-Aged Readers

Lois believes in using a variety of texts with her first graders. Magazines are but one she regularly uses. To make sure that all students have copies of magazines, she has a classroom subscription to *Time for Kids*. In addition to individual student copies of the magazine, there is an enlarged version (i.e., big book) of each issue that she uses for whole-group instruction.

It is October (Children's Magazine Month) and students are learning about spiders. It just so happens that spiders are the focus of the most recent volume of *Time for Kids*. Lois decides to use this volume to her best advantage. She will use the issue to teach students about magazine features, with an emphasis on picture captions and spiders simultaneously. She begins the whole-class lesson by asking, "What do you know about spiders?" As students share their ideas, she writes them on a chart that resembles a spider web. She writes each idea on a different line of the web. She then asks her students what they already know about magazines. Again, she writes their ideas on a chart large enough for all to see.

Now that students are focused on both spiders and magazines, Lois shows the children the big book version of *Time for Kids*. She calls attention to the cover, pictures, and captions beneath the pictures. She then reads the magazine to the students. After this reading, she has students take a look at their spider web chart and add any ideas that they learned from the reading. She closes this part of the lesson by telling students that magazines contain much information and that magazines are written in a specific way. She points to the picture captions and tells students that authors provide these captions so that readers can know more about what the picture is supposed to show and to help them to better comprehend. She also tells them that looking at pictures and reading the captions is a good way to get warmed up for reading. Finally, she tells them that when they read in small groups with her, each will receive a copy of the magazine and they will practice learning how to read picture captions.

The lesson continues with Lois teaching students in small groups of five. Prior to meeting with students, she has written five different picture captions from the magazine on index cards and has placed these in a can. She follows the same process with each group. That is, when a group arrives at the group reading area, she tells students that they will now have some time to read the spider magazine on their own. She distributes a copy of the spider magazine to each group member. She then invites students in turn to select a picture caption from the can and tells them to match their caption with the corresponding one in their magazine. "That is the picture caption you will read to yourselves, and I am here to help you if you need my help," she says. She provides students time to silently read their captions. Once all students are finished reading, they talk about their pictures. They then write one new or interesting idea they have learned about spiders.

Using Magazines with Older Elementary-Aged Readers

Dan's observations have helped him to see that his fourth graders enjoy reading magazines. He decides to use their interest in magazines to his best advantage. He will use them to call students' attention to the different types of text in magazines and show students how to skim to locate specific information. He begins the lesson with the whole class by telling students he's noticed that they read magazines during their independent reading time. He continues by asking questions such as, "So when you read your magazines, what do you do? Do you read every article? Do you look at the advertisements? Do you read the picture captions? Do you read it in order, or do you skip around?"

Students are quick to provide insights. Michael takes the lead. "I usually look through the whole magazine and then go back to what I want to read more carefully."

Another student explains, "I usually read the advertisements and look at the pictures first and I usually read the magazine backwards because it seems easier when holding the magazine."

After listening to several volunteers' responses, Dan capitalizes on their comments by stating, "So magazines can be read in many different ways. Today I want to focus on something you seem to sometimes do without realizing it. When you glance at pictures or look through your magazine to find specific information, you are *skimming*. Skimming is very helpful for readers because it saves much time and helps them identify what they want to know. This is a skill we use when reading magazines, but it is also useful when reading other types of texts. We're going to practice skimming during guided reading using these magazines." He holds up several copies of *Zoobook*. Each issue focuses on a different animal.

The lesson continues with Dan teaching students in small groups of six. A pile of six *Zoobook* magazines is in the center of the table. After students are settled, Dan provides them with directions. "You will need to select one magazine from the center of the table. To save time, simply take the magazine that is on the top of the pile." He provides students with time to select their magazines. "Now here's what you need to do with your magazine within two minutes. Skim through your magazine and locate one fact about your particular animal." He looks at his watch and tells students to begin. Once the two minutes have lapsed, he calls "Stop" and gives each student time to share what he or she discovered. He then has students rotate their magazines to the left and has them repeat the process, providing assistance as needed.

Sample Titles

As already mentioned, there are numerous magazines appropriate for children. *Magazines for Kids and Teens* (Stoll 1997) is one resource for obtaining a compilation of titles. Better yet, go to www.magsonthenet.com to see a list of the most recently published children's magazines, along with prices and ordering information. The following chart shows some sample literary magazines, along with their the age range, subject, and contact information.

Title	Age Range	Subject	Contact Information
Ladybug	2–6	Stories, poems, songs, games, adventures	Carus Publishing PO Box 7433 Red Oak, IA 51591–4433 Ph: 800–827–0227
Shoofly: An Audiomagazine for Children	3–7	Poetry, literature, storytelling, songs	Shoofly PO Box 1237 Carrboro, NC 27510 Ph: 800–919–9989
Stone Soup: The Magazine by Young Writers and Artists	6–13	Writing and art by children	Children's Art Foundation PO Box 83 Santa Cruz, CA 95063 Ph: 800–447–4569

Title	Age Range	Subject	Contact Information
Storyworks	8–12	Literature (also includes student-written book reviews)	Scholastic, Inc. 555 Broadway New York, NY 10012 Ph: 212–343–6333
Faces	8–14	World cultures	Cobblestone Publishing, Inc. 7 School Street Peterborough, NH 03458 Ph: 603–924–7380
Cricket	9–14	Fiction, nonfiction, art	Carus Publishing PO Box 7433 Red Oak, IA 51591–4433 Ph: 800–827–0227
The Claremont Review	13–19	Literature, poetry, and fiction; students also invited to submit writing	The Claremont Review Publishers 4980 Wesley Road Victoria, BC Canada V8Y 1Y9 Ph: 604–658–5221

Some Additional Considerations

OK, we admit it. We are magazine advocates. And as our explanation in this chapter shows, there is good reason. Nonetheless, here are some additional considerations to better ensure your magazine success.

First, while a classroom subscription to a given magazine can be advantageous, it may or may not be necessary depending on how you intend to use the magazine. If you see the magazine as a way of providing your students with additional reading material at home, then having their own copy is essential and would lead to a classroom subscription. If, however, you want to use magazines as one type of literature during independent reading time, then a classroom subscription in which every student obtains a copy is not essential. Instead, as single copies of an issue arrive, these can be stored in a basket or magazine holder with the corresponding label (e.g., *Stone Soup*). Interested students can then access these issues during independent reading time.

Second, just as with other print material, not all magazines are created equal. That is, some, such as those featured in this chapter, contain much information that is sure to broaden students' knowledge about world events and improve their literacy skills. Others, such as *Nickelodeon,* are sure to delight some children yet are often filled with several advertisements aimed at selling products just too good to resist. Both can have their place in the classroom and both can serve as learning tools. As teachers, we are more inclined to purchase those that have more content than advertisements to use in one of several ways (see previous examples and the two scenarios that follow). On the other hand, students may bring to class other more popular magazines that are weighted on the side of advertisements. They can read these magazines during independent reading time (Remember that bad breath is better than no breath! Also remember that *good* is a relative term. See page 19). However, as teachers, we might decide to use some of the advertisements as a catalyst for teaching students something about propaganda techniques. We might also use them to help students to discover for themselves the validity of the claims of some advertisements. For example, hair shampoo is a big topic these days, and several manufacturers of shampoo products have exploited the issue. Different students could try different products and chart results to determine whether or not the claims are true and which is the best buy.

Third, as teachers ourselves, we know firsthand that monetary resources can be limited. For whatever reason, school district personnel spend tremendous amounts of money on textbooks, leaving little for children's literature titles and other print material such as magazines. More teachers than not spend large sums of their own money on books for their classroom libraries. Don't believe us? Attend your state reading conference or a national reading conference and see for yourself. You're sure to hear from more than one teacher, "I just have to have this title for my collection. I'll have to sneak it into the house!"

But the money can only go so far. Fortunately, there are other available resources. The parent-teacher association is but one. Many times members of associations such as these are looking for projects that will help better children's education. Providing them with a rationale along with a list of desired magazines and ordering information is a sure way to get them involved.

Local and national business partners are yet another source. Starbucks is a perfect example. Beyond helping millions of Americans stay caffeine-alert, the company also is interested in community-based projects, as its brochure attests (available in most stores). Talking to the store manager is a first step in securing funds for magazines.

Some state department of education officials provide small grants aimed at helping teachers broaden their instructional materials. Contacting these agencies is another way to obtain additional magazine funding.

Finally, involving parents and students alike is a sure way to get magazines into the classroom. You might consider providing parents with a list of magazines that you would like to have for the classroom during an open house meeting. Providing them with the cost, reasons for the specific magazine, and how the magazine will benefit their children's education can help entice parents to contribute. And what about the students? Some of them, like the young boy Michael Opitz saw in the airport and wrote about in the introduction, are sure to already have a collection of magazines. Invite them to bring in their old copies for others to read.

Conclusions

Magazines help broaden students' understanding not only of their world but of how reading works. As a result of reading magazines, they become comfortable with magazine text structure and begin to understand that different texts can and should be read in different ways. When they read magazines both in and out of school, they begin to get a better grasp of reading as an activity that serves valuable purposes throughout their lives, regardless of setting. And let's remember the power of student interest in terms of reading. While magazines are far different from other texts, they do provide students with much practice that better ensures that they will be able to read other texts. As such, they serve a purpose in helping children become skilled and willing readers.

Websites

http://childmagmonth.org provides an alphabetical list of kids magazines as well as a list of age-appropriate magazines. It also provides ideas for how to use magazines and an explanation about Children's Magazine Month: what it is, why it was created, and who created it.

www.nationalgeographic.com/kids provides a wealth of ideas about *National Geographic Kids Magazine*. It also provides specific ideas for parents and suggested activities that can be completed at home or at school.

http://kids.discovery.com offers suggestions that relate to *Kids Discovery* magazine. It includes games and puzzles as well as a parent newsletter.

http://www.cobblestoneonline.net provides a detailed background of Cobblestone and Cricket, divisions of Carus Publishing. It also features a listing of magazines they publish, which span the ages from birth to high school (*Appleseeds, Ask, Babybug, Calliope, Cicada, Click, Cobblestone, Cricket, Dig, Faces, Ladybug, Muse, Odyssey,* and *Spider*). Free teacher guides accompany most magazines. And, yes, the authors of the website group the magazines by subject as well as grade level. You can also discover publishing guidelines for authors and illustrators of all ages.

http://www.nal.usda.gov/kids/scimags.htm is sure to please those who are interested in science magazines. This site provides a listing of numerous science magazines such as *Science Weekly, Dragonfly,* and *National Geographic World.* Complete contact information is provided, as is the intended age level(s) for each magazine.

http://archaeology.about.com/od/magazinesforchildren provides a list of several archaeology magazines for children. Background information about archaeology-related terms is also provided.

CHAPTER 3

Poetry

Listen to Mother play. She practices and practices a piece, and sometimes magic happens and it seems the music starts to breathe. It sends a shiver through you. You can't explain it, really; it's a mystery. Well, when words do that, we call it poetry. —Michael Bedard, *Emily*

There is an elusiveness about poetry that makes it defy precise definition. It is not so much what it is that is important, as how it makes us feel.

—Charlotte Huck, Barbara Kiefer, Susan Hepler, and Janet Hickman,
Children's Literature in the Elementary School

A Brief Description

In Michael Bedard's book *Emily* (1992), a young girl wonders whether her neighbor Emily Dickinson is lonely. Her father tries to allay her concerns by reminding his daughter that Miss Dickinson has her sister, her plants, and her poetry. When asked, "What is poetry?" her father uses music as a way of explaining this elusive art form. While there is an elusive quality to poetry, it is probably a stretch to say that it defies definition. In her poem "Things," Eloise Greenfield (1978) reminds us that poems are much more lasting than some things in life. She poetically explains that if you write a poem, you will have it long after the candy you bought and the sand house you made are gone.

Harris and Hodges define poetry as "literature in metrical form" (1995, 189). They add that poems are compositions "in which word images are selected and expressed to create powerful, often beautiful impressions in the listener or reader" (189). Even Huck and her colleagues explain that poetry "requires a more highly structured patterning of words. Each word must be chosen with care for both sound and meaning" (2005, 359). This careful word choice is often used in a manner that plays with language to convey the pleasure of sound and language (Nodelman and Reimer 2003).

Poetry is often defined by distinguishing it from prose. Poetry is verse language, presented in forms without attention to the conventions of narrative texts. Mechanics of traditional punctuation, capitalization, sentence grammar, and text structure that govern prose text are not required conventions for poetry. Poems not only look different from traditional stories but also can look quite different from each other. Meaning in poetic forms is composed and comprehended in ways that are quite different from the ways used in prose texts.

Poetry is a complex genre. It includes major forms like epic, lyric, and dramatic poems. Teachers and students may be more familiar with other forms, like limericks and haiku, with set formats. Students learn that haiku are composed with three lines of five syllables, seven syllables, and five syllables. Limericks contain a rhyme scheme of AABBA. Most well-known poetry is organized into stanzas; however, one cannot fall into the trap of thinking that all poems contain stanzas. For instance, concrete poems don't have stanzas. In concrete poems, the words themselves are formatted to create a visual of what the poem is about. These different types of formats further define poetry.

Why Use Them?

As a complex genre, poetry has many important characteristics we can use to engage readers. One of the most attractive attributes of poetry is the opportunity to play with language. The flow of the language in poetry is its greatest attraction. Matthew starts to move to the rhythm of the poem as if he's listening to a song. M. C. Helldorfer captures this effectively in the book *Got to Dance* (2004). Each event in a little girl's day with her grandfather becomes a moment for a poetic, rhythmic celebration. This rhythm is connected to the lyrical quality of poetry. Maybe one reason for introducing poetry to students is to invite them to just enjoy the sound of the language being used within the poem. Through rhythm, rhyme, alliteration, repetition, onomatopoeia, and nonsense words, poetry enables us to enjoy the way language sounds.

While enjoying the language play might be an important aspect of poetry, there are other benefits as well. Pointing out the importance of reading poetry aloud, Jacobs and Tunnell observe "poetry really is meant to be heard more than read silently; the avenue to poetry appreciation for many students is the oral highway" (2004, 197). The rhythm of the poem also helps guide the reader to feel the language. Using the rhythm, readers can begin to work on reading fluency, another benefit of poetry. The oral reading of poetry is a perfect opportunity to read with greater speed, accuracy, and expression. The inherent rhythm of poetic language actually helps the student with pacing. When Matthew reads "The Owl and the Pussycat" (Lear 1996) to classes, for example, his rate increases because he likes to hear the poem read quickly.

Economy of language is another benefit of poetry. For example, in the classic Jeff Moss poem "Punishment" (1991), Moss conveys his meaning in five words. (Hint: It involves eating cauliflower!) In another Moss poem, the title "What People Don't Want to See at the Dinner Table" (1991) is actually longer than the poem, which answers the question in four words. (Hint: It involves chewed food!) Since poems must get their message across with relatively few words, they can be very effective in conveying visual and other sensory images. Poetry encourages visualization, whether it is the park bench in the winter in *Snowy Benches,* by Aileen Fisher (1980), or the fence in *The Picket Fence,* by David McCord (1997). Poetry often allows the reader to visualize more efficiently. Poems in Arnold Adoff's *Chocolate Dreams* (1989) quickly surface sensory experiences beyond images. Can you already smell and taste the subject of his poem just by knowing the title?

Another reason for using poetry is the emotional punch that it packs. Huck et al. describe this best: "Poetry communicates experience by appealing to both the thoughts and feelings of its reader" (2005, 360). Poetry invites the reader to feel the same emotions it's describing. Instead of analyzing a poem, students should be invited to discuss how the poem makes them feel. As Janeczko notes: "I want my students to stretch their intellects when they read a poem, to let their hearts grow" (2003, 13). In order for this to happen, readers need to delve into the feelings and emotions that the poem evokes. Discussing the emotions in poems can help with deeper reading.

Whether it is the study of language within poems, or the images poetry evokes, poetry needs a place in the classroom reading program. It plays with language; encourages experimentation with expressive, fluent oral reading;

and evokes strong emotional responses. Let's look at six more reasons for using poetry to meet the needs of the many readers in a classroom.

To Better Motivate All Readers

Poetry has a power to reach readers who might surprise you. Consider the motivational profiles; poetry might be especially good for those students who say, "I'm not very good at reading." Readers with self-efficacy issues may find that the way language flows in poetry helps them read more smoothly, quickly, and accurately. Through language play with rhythm, rhyme, alliteration, and onomatopoeia, these students will discover that there is a fun *sound* to poetry. Working with the different elements of poetry will help readers gain confidence in their reading. The rhythm of a poem can help readers hear how the words might be read. Onomatopoeia can help children accentuate sounds and words while reading the poems. In the end, hearing their interpretation of a poem or others' positive reactions to their interpretation will show readers that they indeed *are* good at reading. As they watch their confidence, competence, and comfort levels grow, students will discover that they can be successful readers.

Poetry can also be inviting to those who say, "Reading is not very important to me." These readers are usually drawn to texts that link to other priorities of their lives. One way to encourage students who fall into this profile is to invite them to make the connection between poetry and their favorite songs. One of Matthew's brothers pointed this out to him recently in a conversation about one of their favorite groups. He told Matthew that the song used the familiar rhyme scheme of ABABC. Mathew had never thought about that before, and thought his brother was out of his mind. After he hung up the phone, he listened to the song, and sure enough, it did follow the same rhyme scheme his brother had described. Pointing out such similarities to students will help them see that poetry has real-life connections for them. Capitalizing on something that already interests them can better motivate these reluctant readers.

To Shed Light on the Complexity of Reading

One of the major complaints about poetry is that students are commonly asked to identify the one main theme of a poem. Focusing on finding the one right meaning for the poem often leads to frustration. Not only does it tend to distract from the beauty of the *language* in the poem, but it also denies how reader factors affect the interpretation of the poem. We each bring different backgrounds to a poem. Since we all have varied schemata that we bring to a text, it's important to show readers that there can be multiple interpretations of a poem (Certo 2004; Janeczko 2003). An example that Matthew likes to share with his classes is the punk-rock song by Green Day "Good Riddance: The Time of My Life." He questions whether Billie Joe Armstrong sat down and said, "I think I'll write a song that will be played at every prom and graduation across the country." He had his own reasons for writing this song, but it obviously connected for probably many different reasons with many people.

To Expand Children's Understandings of the Variety of Text Genres and Structures

How do children learn about the genre of poetry and the structures of verse language if it rarely shows up in the school reading programs? Only by exposing students to a wide variety of poetic forms can we help them begin to learn how these texts are composed and comprehended. We need to be intentional about helping children explore many different types of poems. As noted, poems structured in stanzas should be approached differently than poems structured loosely in single words and short phrases. Epic poems organized around narrative stories require a different set of comprehension strategies than the haiku of Japanese masters. For some readers who haven't seen poems in these formats, reading them can be a bit intimidating, especially at first. By exposing children to the different poetry formats like the traditional stanzas found in such poems as "Things" (Greenfield 1978) or the free-verse structures of poems in *Chocolate Dreams* (Adoff 1989), students can build their confidence with the format. The same can be said for teachers. Janeczko writes: "The more poetry we read the more comfortable we will be with it, and the more confident we will feel bringing in poems for students to share" (2003, 16).

We are starting to see the convergence of poetry with traditional genres like realistic and historical fiction. Authors are starting to write novels in verse. Karen Hesse did this in her Newbery award–winning novel *Out of the Dust* (1999). Hesse writes in free verse to tell the story of a young girl's struggle to survive the dust bowl. She uses few words to create vivid and strong images. *Make Lemonade,* by Virginia Euwer Wolff (1994), and *Bronx Masquerade,* by Nikki Grimes (2002), are two additional examples of novels in verse. Finally, Sharon Creech also used free verse to write her two novels

Love That Dog (2003) and *Heartbeat* (2005). Both are inviting to readers, both through the flow of the language and the story they tell.

Being able to read a novel composed of short poems may be especially attractive to readers in the "I'm not very good at reading" and "Reading is not very important to me" profiles. These readers will find themselves easily engaged in the books, and perhaps even motivated to read more. Michael Ford shared that whenever one of his sons needs to jump-start his recreational reading habit, he always grabs *Love That Dog*. Recognize, however, that sometimes these novels look deceptively easy because of their format when they actually require a more sophisticated level of interpretation and response.

To Make More Texts Acceptable and Accessible in and out of School

For one reason or another, poetry sometimes gets a bad rap (pun intended). It could be a negative experience with poetry, or exposure to specific types and forms (the classics) that students were taught in earlier grades. Whatever the reason, it's important to help students see that poetry is all around them. From commercial jingles to birthday card greetings, from posters held up to cheer on a favorite team to the lyrics of favorite songs, students live in a world that is filled with verse language. Using song lyrics might be one of the easiest ways to show them. We have seen the idea of bringing rap music into classrooms many times and Smith and Wilhelm (2002) mention this idea in *"Reading Don't Fix No Chevys."* When teachers let students bring music or poems in for a reading lesson, it allows readers to see such things as the use of metaphors in a natural and familiar text. Using student-selected poems is also a good opportunity for teachers to connect with students. While teachers need to be mindful of the song lyrics they include from students, using their music validates student interests.

Making poetry more acceptable in and out of school is important, but so is accessibility. One way to provide access is to have many poetry books on the classroom bookshelves. Fortunately, there are many new poetry titles. *The Blood Hungry Spleen* (Wolf 2003), *Science Verse* (Scieszka and Smith 2004), *Oh No! Where Are My Pants?* (Bennett Hopkins 2005), *Bow Wow, Meow Meow* (Florian 2003), and *Least Things* (Yolen 2003) are just a few. Having picture book poetry texts, novels in verse, and poetry anthologies available in the classroom enables children to access many poets beyond the beloved Shel Silverstein and Jack Prelutsky they may already know.

Making connections between texts is an important strategy that can be fostered easily with poetry. In *Love That Dog,* Sharon Creech (2003) uses poems by Robert Frost and Walter Dean Myers as part of the story she tells in her novel written in verse. The title is based on Myers' poem "Love That Boy." Teachers can help readers make connections between the different poems in the book and the poems that the main character, Jack, writes.

Another way text-to-text connections can be taught is by reading poems from multiple texts. Reading a book like *Love That Dog,* we can make connections with other poetry books—*Bow Wow, Meow Meow* (Florian 2003), for example—that focus on dogs. Since many anthologies are themed or divided into themes, finding a number of poems that could foster intertextual connections within a topic is fairly easy.

Besides topics and themes, different poems often contain similar uses of language. Metaphors and similes play a big role in poetry. Students can be taught to recognize how two things are being compared in a literary sense in one poem and use that strategy to see how comparisons are being made in other texts. Another common feature of poetry is figurative language. Many poems and verse are full of clichés such as "blanket of snow" and "quiet as a mouse." We can point out similarities in common figurative language and the language used in poems. Similar images also show up in different poems. Comparing and contrasting these elements across different poems will show students how what they learn from one text can be used to help them respond to another text.

One category of poems—innovations and parodies—requires the reader to make intertextual connections to appreciate the poems at their deepest level. For appreciation of these poems, the reader needs to make connections to the poems upon which they are based. In *Science Verse* (Scieszka and Smith 2004), familiar poems and songs are recast to present scientific concepts ranging from black holes to evolution. Karen Shapiro rewrites many of the classic poems to convey aspects of children's lives in her book *Because I Could Not Stop My Bike and Other Poems* (2005). Imagine Elizabeth Barrette Browning's poem redone as a salute to ketchup—"How do I love you? Let me count the ways . . ." Alan Katz has turned to classic songs to find the material for his books *Take Me Out of the Bathtub and Other Silly, Dilly Songs* (2001), *I'm Still Here in the Bathtub* (2003), and *Where Did They*

Hide My Presents? (2005). Each book is filled with parodies updating the classic verses as songs for today's children's lives.

To Address the Oversimplification of Leveling Systems Often Used to Determine Which Books Children Should Read

Jim Trelease once called *Where the Sidewalk Ends* (Silverstein 1974) the most popular book in schools. His evidence? He said if you asked teachers and librarians which book was stolen the most by kids from classrooms and libraries, they would say *Where the Sidewalk Ends.* Shel Silverstein is probably one of the most commonly read poets in children's literature. Can you identify the reading level of his books? Probably not. That's the beauty of poetry: it can cross many different reading levels. Whether it is a picture book, in an anthology, in a large collection like Silverstein's, or a novel in verse, there is a poem for every reader. In fact, one of the advantages of anthologies is you can hand struggling readers poems that are accessible in books that are also acceptable (carry no stigma).

Remember, though, that just because a poem contains few words does not mean it's an easy poem that's below a given reading level. If we only base reading level on the number of words in the poem, we are selling poetry short. Haiku, for example, uses only seventeen syllables but is quite complex. "Haiku is deceiving in that the form appears simple yet it requires much from its reader" (Huck et al. 2005). While a reader may be able to call out the words in a haiku, it doesn't necessarily mean he'll be able to understand what he's read. A format such as limerick may have a higher readability level because it is longer, but because it is more whimsical and fun, it may be easier to comprehend. An overemphasis on trying to level poetry prevents many readers from discovering the joy of poetry and from practicing the different reading skills discussed in this chapter.

How Might They Be Used?

Read-aloud: Clearly, one of the best times to use poetry is during read-aloud time. Poems are short but whole. In a relatively few minutes, a teacher can share a poem or two with students and the whole texts will be in their heads. As a first-grade teacher, Michael Ford discovered the power of reading aloud poetry to his students. Armed with two well-worn copies of *Where the Sidewalk Ends* (1974) and *A Light in the Attic* (1981), he started every day reading aloud a poem from Shel Silverstein. After he read through the poem once, students would join in the rereading, adding some actions or interaction, and then he'd read an old favorite requested by the class. Mike knew that he had uncovered something valuable when his children moved on to the second grade. The veteran second-grade teacher asked him, "What did you do with poetry last year? I have never had a group of kids before who were so excited about reading and writing poems." It was clear that the few minutes spent sharing poems during the read-aloud time with his class was powerful and memorable.

Like Mike, other teachers have discovered the benefit from reading a few poems aloud every day. A teacher enrolled in one of Matthew's graduate classes shared this story about poetry reading in her classroom: She often read a poem or two to her students each day, that is, until she felt pressured by mandated tests. She then stopped reading the poems so that she could devote more time to students' test preparation. One day, a student asked her about it and told her how much he missed the poetry reading. Other students expressed the same concern. After thinking about their comments and her purposes for reading poetry aloud in the first place, she resumed reading poetry, tests or no tests. As this story shows, even when teachers are crunched for time, they can find a few seconds to share a poem with their students. Bruce Lansky's *Funny Little Poems for Funny Little People* (2002) provides a wealth of short poems. We are not at a loss for short poems to read aloud regardless of the teaching position. If you are a resource teacher and only have your students for a relatively short amount of time or an administrator dropping into classrooms, equipping yourself with poems you can share quickly and enthusiastically with students is a sure way to model the power of reading.

Shared reading: Poet and illustrator Ashley Bryant started an early morning presentation with an echo reading of "Things" by Eloise Greenfield (1978). The audience quickly matched his enthusiasm and expression while echoing the poem. Remember that at least one teaching point provides the focus for a shared reading experience. In this case it was clear that Ashley's goal was to model reading with expression and excitement. Hearing the audience repeat the intonations that he used helped demonstrate that he had met his goal.

You can capture that same excitement in your reading programs. Friendly, familiar poems provide many opportunities to teach components ranging from concepts of print to sophisticated strategies for comprehension and composition. The key is always making sure that poems don't merely serve an instructional purpose in the classroom. We don't want to rip the heart out of a poem just for the sake of using it to teach a skill or strategy.

The following top-down lesson provides a frame for developing a shared reading lesson. Let's look at how the lesson flows:

1. Share the poem aloud with your students.

2. Once the poem is in their heads (and hearts), structure interactive activities that transfer the oral language of the poem from the teacher to the students. Here are three suggestions:

   ■ Decide on actions to use with the poem and invite students to act it out as you share it aloud.

   ■ Ask students to chime in with you on predictable parts.

   ■ Ask students to echo increasingly larger parts of the poem as you say it with them. Invite students to say increasingly larger parts of the poem with you in a choral reading.

3. Once the language is in the heads of the students, bring on the print. Enlarge the words of the poem for all to see. Begin to match the oral language to the written words. Consider having students do a choral reading while you or a student points to the words as they are read. You could also have students perform the poem readers' theater style, which would also ensure that students are connecting the oral and written words. Think about having students read with buddies. Then, too, they can read the poem independently

4. Move the poem or a chunk of it over to the pocket chart and have students work with it in one of three ways:

   ■ *Work with the text at the line level*—Give them matching sentence strips and have them place the strips over each line in the poem.

   ■ *Work with the text at the word level*—Provide word cards for the poem and have students match the cards to the words in the displayed poem. Students can place the words right on top of the words in the chart.

   ■ *Work with the text at the word-part level*—Cut up some of the words and encourage students to put them together. They can use the displayed poem to check their word constructions.

5. Create materials based on the poem that provide additional practice with reading and writing. For example, students might illustrate a book that showcases the poem. They might also decide to act out the poem and to perform it to interested others. You could also do a text

innovation of the poem by using the basic structure of the poem and having students fill in different words.

Remember that in this top-down shared reading lesson, the instruction begins with appreciation, enjoyment, and understanding of the poem. Once the poem is familiar and friendly, it should be able to withstand a bit of analysis and strategy work without losing its appeal to the students.

Guided reading: One of the nice things about poetry is that it's inexpensive to give each student a copy of the same poem. With poetry you don't always need to have multiple copies of a book to lead a guided reading group. In addition, as we described in the intertextuality section, different poems at approximately the same level can be chosen around a specific theme (e.g., weather, animals, school) so that each student can have something different to read during guided reading time. Creating this type of a poetry text set lends itself to the possibility of facilitating discussion and response beyond a single text during guided reading. Using poetry during guided reading time allows many opportunities to help students study a variety of aspects found within the poems. For example, the guided reading lesson might focus on how stanzas can help children understand the process of phrasing when reading. Each student could have a different poem and could look at how the poem is divided into different stanzas, thus encouraging phrasing to be done at those specific breaks the poet has chosen.

Another lesson might encourage readers to look at different aspects of language. Poetry is full of metaphors and similes. A guided reading lesson could help readers see the comparisons being made in their poems. Pointing out the signal words such as *like* and *as,* students can share how two things are being compared in a literary sense. Yet another focus could be on figurative language. Many poems and verses are full of clichés such as "blanket of snow" and "quiet as a mouse." Teachers can help students point out similarities in figurative language across poems or contrast multiple meanings of words and phrases used differently in different texts. Since each reader has a different poem, the common theme allows the students to share their poems and see how they're related as well. Notice how this type of lesson pushes guided reading beyond attention to the micro level of the text (words, sentences, and literal-level comprehension) and begins to help students focus attention at the macro level of the text (ideas, themes, and strategies for response).

Independent reading: Our personal copies of *Where the Sidewalk Ends* are well worn. Not only have we gone through it again and again to read poems to our classes, but our students (both elementary and college) have read it again and again. By having access to many different poetry texts in the class-room, students are always able to read from this genre during independent reading time. Exposure to the different structures of poetry described throughout this chapter helps students gain confidence and familiarity with the genre. They will then be more willing to pick it up and read it on their own.

Besides inviting students to add poetry to their independent reading habits, you can also have them use poetry for independent work. For example, any of the projects mentioned earlier as final outcomes from a top-down shared reading experience (e.g., self-illustrated books, performances, innovations) can be done as independent work. In their book *Reaching Readers: Flexible and Innovative Strategies for Guided Reading*, Opitz and Ford (2001) describe a poetry folder they suggest using to keep students engaged in powerful work while away from the teacher and the guided reading group she or he is working with. The folder contains a number of activities based on each poem. For example, each student receives a hard copy of the poems shared during the large-group activities. During independent reading time, the student knows that he can practice reading a hard copy of a poem to improve his fluency or speech-to-print matching. He can work with a buddy or a small group to practice a choral reading of the poem in two or three voices. The folder might also contain directions for how the student can turn the poem into a project that will lead to even more reading and writing. Students might create a self-illustrated book based on the poem or contribute to a page to help create a classroom mural based on the stanzas from the poem.

Using Poetry with Younger Elementary-Aged Readers

Jane, a first-grade teacher, had very positive experiences learning poetry when she herself was in elementary school. It was so positive that she studied English in college and memorized poems on her own. She wants to help share this love of poetry with her own students. One of the main ways Jane sees how she can do this with her first graders is to show them the beauty of language and how it sounds within poems. She collects as many poetry books as she can that use rhyme and adds them to her classroom library. Each day she shares one or two of the poems with her class. After she orally introduces a number of poems to her students, the poems become very familiar to her students. She picks one of the favorite poems and asks her students to listen for rhyming words. She tells her class to signal with a thumbs-up sign when they hear a pair of rhyming words. She repeats the poem with a strong emphasis on the first rhyming pair. She models a thumbs-up signal and then reveals that she heard a rhyming pair. She restates the pair, separating the onset and rime, revealing how the words have the same endings (rimes) but different beginnings (onsets). She also identifies a few other words that rhyme with the pair. She tells her class to listen for the next rhyming pair and signal when they hear it. She continues with the poem, emphasizing the next rhyming pair. She watches as a number of thumbs go up. She invites those with thumbs up to tell a buddy what rhyming pair they heard. When asked, the class chimes in collectively to reveal the rhyming pair. The children work together with Jane to separate the onsets and rimes and then they generate a few more partners for the rhyming pair. Jane practices rhyming pairs with the class until she senses that her students are successful at identifying the rhymes without much support.

Jane then turns to the poem she has written on a piece of chart paper. She leads the class in a shared reading of the poem so that the students can watch the words as they say the poem. She grabs her special pointer and helps the children visually track the words on the chart as they are saying them aloud. She hits the rhyming words with her pointer just a little harder than the others. She shows the students how the words in the first rhyming pair also look alike. She shows how the ends of the words look similar, especially when you take away the letter that makes the first sound. She then thinks aloud and shows how she can spell some other words that rhyme with the pair by using the same visual pattern. She continues to move through the poem with her pointer and asks her children to use their thumbs-up signal when they see another rhyming pair. As the pairs are discovered, Jane guides the children through looking at the words' similarities and differences. She helps them use the patterns to spell other words in the rhyming family, recording the words on a separate sheet of chart paper as the children say them. She also seizes a few additional teachable moments when a few words surfaced by her children end up being exceptions to the patterns. After using the favorite poem for word work, Jane invites them to recite the poem without interruptions so they can enjoy the flow of the language found in the poem and read it fluently.

Using Poetry with Older Elementary-Aged Readers

Charlie knows that teaching poetry might be a challenge with older readers because he hasn't see his students reading much poetry. While his experiences with poetry seem rather neutral, he wants to inspire his fifth graders, especially the boys, to try their hand at poetry. Charlie recently discovered Sharon Creech's book *Love That Dog* (2003), a chapter book written in short verses. It seems like the perfect text to share with his reluctant readers of poetry. The main character in this book, Jack, is a self-professed hater of poetry. Jack seems like the perfect character to introduce to Charlie's reluctant writers of poetry. He uses the first part of the book in a shared lesson with his students. He talks about how Jack is facing an assignment to write a poem (much like they are) and how he faces this challenge by actually writing a couple of poems in his journal about his disinterest in the genre:

> I don't want to
> because boys
> don't write poetry.
>
> Girls do.

> And

> I tried.
> Can't do it.
> Brain's empty.

The first part of the book and Jack's initial attempts at poetry set up a discussion with Charlie's students. They start with a number of text-to-self connections as Charlie invites them to think about whether they ever felt like Jack. They look at text-to-text connections as Charlie invites them to compare Jack's first attempts at poetry with other familiar poems. The students engage in a heated debate about the quality of Jack's poems; some use examples to praise Jack's work and others use examples to criticize his attempts. Charlie invites his students to experiment with their attempts at poetry by writing in their journals. He reminds them that if they need to get their writing started, they might consider doing what Jack did, which was write a poem that captured his feelings about having to write poems. Charlie also points out that they can tell any story that they may have written in prose as a story in verse, like Sharon Creech does in *Love That Dog*.

Charlie finds that many of the scenes in *Love That Dog* provide appropriate material for lessons during writing workshop time. He shares a section of the book where Jack's teacher continues to try to get Jack excited about poetry by introducing him to Walter Dean Myers' work. Jack falls in love with one poem by Myers, "Love That Boy," which inspires him to write his own. Both the poem by Myers and the poem written by Jack provide catalysts for talking about what elements make up a quality poem. Charlie points to the techniques actually used by Myers and talks about how his work might influence the students in much the same way that Jack is influenced when attempting his own poetry using free verse. At the same time, Charlie can pull back and show his students the techniques Sharon Creech is using in telling the broader story of *Love That Dog*. The novel sets up multiple opportunities for pointing out how others express their emotions through poetry—you can see it in the poetry of Myers, the poetry of the main character, and in the novel as a whole.

The use of this novel allows Charlie to expand the types of poetry and poets he has been able to introduce to his students. He wants them to know that poetry is one way to express themselves and their ideas when they are writing. He capitalizes on his students' attraction to the verse novel *Love That Dog* and introduces another verse novel by Creech called *Heartbeat* (2005). That leads to other verse novels, like Nikki Grimes' *Bronx Masquerade* (2002) and Karen Hesse's *Out of the Dust* (1999), as well as the biography *Carver* (Nelson 2001). *Love That Dog* also leads to other novels by Sharon Creech and Walter Dean Myers. By exposing students to a number of authors who use both prose and poetry in their writings, Charlie hopes to encourage his students to experiment with more forms in their own writing.

Sample Titles

Poems for More Than One Voice

Title	Author	Publisher/Year ISBN	Suggested Grade Levels
You Read to Me, I'll Read to You: Very Short Stories to Read Together	Hoberman	Megan Tingley/2001 0316363502	pre-K–3
You Read to Me, I'll Read to You: Very Short Mother Goose Tales to Read Together	Hoberman	Megan Tingley/2005 0316144312	1–4
I Am Phoenix: Poems for Two Voices	Fleischman	HarperTrophy/1989 0064460924	4–8
Joyful Noise: Poems for Two Voices	Fleischman	HarperTrophy/1992 0064460932	4–8
Big Talk: Poems for Four Voices	Fleischman	Candlewick/2000 0763606367	5–8

Teaching Forms and Types of Poetry

Title	Author	Publisher/Year ISBN	Suggested Grade Levels
A Poke in the I: A Collection of Concrete Poems	Janeczko and Raschka	Candlewick/2001 0763606618	K–3
A Kick in the Head: An Everyday Guide to Poetic Forms	Janeczko and Raschka	Candlewick/2005 0763606626	4–6

Comparing and Contrasting Contemporary and Classic Poems

Title	Author	Publisher/Year ISBN	Suggested Grade Levels
Because I Could Not Stop My Bike and Other Poems	Shapiro	Charlesbridge/2005 1580890350	3–5
Science Verse	Scieszka and Smith	Viking Juvenile/2004 0670910570	3–5
Here in Harlem: Poems in Many Voices	Myers	Holiday House/2004 0823418537	6–8

Song Parodies

Title	Author	Publisher/Year ISBN	Suggested Grade Levels
I'm Still Here in the Bathtub: Brand New Silly Dilly Songs	Katz	Margaret K. McElderry/2003 0689845510	K–5
Take Me Out of the Bathtub and Other Silly, Dilly Songs	Katz	Margaret K. McElderry/2001 0689829035	K–5
Where Did They Hide My Presents? Silly Dilly Christmas Songs	Katz	Margaret K. McElderry/2005 0689862148	K–5

Fun Books

Title	Author	Publisher/Year ISBN	Suggested Grade Levels
Got to Dance	Helldorfer	Doubleday/2004 0385326289	pre-K–1
Pigs Rock	Davis Jones	Viking Books/2003 0670035815	pre-K–1

Title	Author	Publisher/Year ISBN	Suggested Grade Levels
Funny Little Poems for Funny Little People	Lansky	Meadowbrook/2002 0689024541	K–2
Least Things: Poems About Small Natures	Yolen	Boyds Mills/2003 1590780981	K–5
The Ocean Is . . .	Kranking	Henry Holt/2003 0805070974	1–3
Bow Wow, Meow Meow: It's Rhyming Cats and Dogs	Florian	Harcourt Children's/2003 0152163956	1–5
Oh, No! Where Are My Pants? And Other Disasters: Poems	Bennett Hopkins	HarperCollins/2005 068817860X	2–5
The Butterfly Jar	Moss	Bantam/1989 0553057049	2–6
The Other Side of the Door	Moss	Bantam/1991 0553072595	3–4
The Blood Hungry Spleen and Other Poems About Our Parts	Wolf	Candlewick/2003 076361565X	3–5
Snow, Snow: Winter Poems for Children	Yolen	Dutton Juvenile/2002 0525469494	4–6
The Song Shoots Out of My Mouth: A Celebration of Music	Adoff	Dutton Juvenile/2002 052469494	6–8

Poetry Novels

Title	Author	Publisher/Year ISBN	Suggested Grade Levels
Love That Dog	Creech	HarperTrophy/2003 0064409597	3–5
Carver: A Life in Poems	Nelson	Front Street/2001 1886910537	4–6
Locomotion	Woodson	Puffin/2004 0142401498	4–6
Out of the Dust	Hesse	Scholastic/1999 0590371258	4–6
Heartbeat	Creech	HarperTrophy/2005 0060540249	4–7

Title	Author	Publisher/Year ISBN	Suggested Grade Levels
Bronx Masquerade	Grimes	Puffin/2003 0142501891	6–8
Make Lemonade	Euwer Wolff	Scholastic Paperbacks/1994 059048141X	6–8
Jinx	Wild	Simon Pulse/2004 0689865414	9–12

Novels About Poetry

Title	Author	Publisher/Year ISBN	Suggested Grade Levels
Emily	Bedard	Doubleday Books for Young Readers/ 1992 0385306970	K–5

Conclusions

Poetry is different from prose. It comes in a variety of formats such as lyrical, limerick, haiku, narrative, and concrete. And while not all students may be comfortable with all types of poems, most enjoy the rhyme and language play poets use to write poetry. Using a variety of poems is one of the best ways to help children extend their understanding of language. Using poetry in one or more ways shows children that it is an acceptable genre, one worth exploring. Having many different poetry books available makes the poems accessible. And, as we show this chapter, there are many ways to make poetry both acceptable and accessible.

Websites

http://gigglepoetry.com offers hundreds of poems for readers to not only read but also rate! Different categories of poems include family poems, favorite poems, and school poems. Not to be missed are the variety of ideas for learning how to write different types of poems and how to do a poetry theater. And if you want information about specific children's poets, this is the place to visit, as the site showcases several with accompanying interviews.

www.kristinegeorge.com provides information about Kristine George, a poet who writes for children. Those who visit this site can find information about the author, her books, teaching guides for some of the books, and activities for children, each based on one of her books.

www.poetryzone.ndirect.co.uk/teacher.htm is a comprehensive website. It offers bibliographies of current poetry titles, classroom resources, and directions for how to write poems.

www.favoritepoem.org provides information about the Favorite Poem Project, which was founded by Robert Pinsky, the thirty-ninth United States poet laureate. One part of this website is specifically designed for teachers and provides an interactive gallery so that they can view favorite poem videos and access poetry lesson plans.

www.onlinepoetryclassroom.org provides much help for any teacher wanting to do a better job of teaching poetry. The site encourages teachers to share ideas and seek help from others, and it provides extensive information about poets and poems.

4

Multilevel Texts

There is no single organizational scheme that we can simply put in place and leave alone.
　　　　　　　　　　　　　—Richard Allington, "The Reading Instruction
　　　　　　　　　　　　　　　　Provided Readers of Differing Reading Ability"

A Brief Description

We know. As if book leveling and the complications that sometimes accompany it aren't enough, here we are adding to the book-leveling complexities by writing about texts that contain more than one level. "What's that? Some books have more than one level?" you ask? That's right! Several authors are writing books that contain more than one story, and each operates independently of the other. And more often than not, the authors write the stories at different difficulty levels. We call these kinds of books *multilevel texts* because that is exactly what they are, and as we show in this chapter, they have much to offer. But, for clarity's sake, we need to note that even though there are children's literature titles that contain secondary text, such as *A Subway for New York* (Weitzman 2005), these are anything but multilevel texts as we define them here. Instead, any book we consider to be multilevel needs to have the following characteristics:

1. *More than one story line is evident and each can stand independently of the other.* That is, the reader can choose which story line to read and can make sense of the text. Some titles contain two story lines (e.g., *One Leaf Rides the Wind*, by Mannis [2002]), whereas others

contain three story lines (e.g., *New York, New York! The Big Apple from A to Z,* by Melmed [2005]).

2. *Different genres (i.e., multigenres) or similar genres are used to write the different story lines.* In *One Leaf Rides the Wind* (Mannis 2002), for example, the author uses haiku to tell about objects a child sees in a Japanese garden, making the text appear as sheer poetry. Upon closer inspection, however, we see that the author also uses nonfiction to provide information about religion or philosophy for each object in the garden. Those who read this nonfiction text will see it as informational text rather than as poetry. On the other hand, in *Alpha, Bravo, Charlie: The Military Alphabet,* Demarest (2005) uses nonfiction for both story lines.

3. *Authors write the different stories with varying difficulty levels.* For example, in *Elephants Can Paint, Too!* Arnold (2005) uses realistic fiction to explain commonalities between humans and animals. The story is in large type, the language is conversational, and captivating, telling pictures provide novice readers with much support as they read the text. Consequently, those who read this story will be able to claim that they have read the book, and they have. However, there is another story in which the author uses nonfiction to explain specific behaviors of elephants. This story is in smaller type and is encapsulated in a green section on the page. Pictures accompany each section. More sophisticated readers will be able to read this story, and in doing so, they, too, will be able to claim that they have read the book, which they have. It just so happens that they read a different story contained in the book.

4. *End matter might exist.* Sometimes authors of multilevel texts go a step further by including additional information in the back of the text (e.g., *Grandma Elephant's in Charge,* by Jenkins [2003]). This information is primarily aimed at extending the story or stories within the text; it rarely can stand on its own (e.g., *Wise Guy: The Life and Philosophy of Socrates,* by Usher [2005]). Therefore, we do not consider this type of information yet another story line. Make no mistake, however. This information is interesting and some or all students might be encouraged to read it.

5. *The texts are authentic.* In other words, the authors write to communicate their ideas to their intended audiences rather than to create a text with controlled vocabulary and use specific words a given number of times. You can purchase these texts in most bookstores.

Why Use Them?

One of Michael Opitz's major goals as a teacher is to ensure that all students feel part of the classroom community. As such, students "experience a sense of being valued and respected: they feel connected to each other" (Kohn 1996, 101). So his number one reason for using multilevel texts is that they facilitate this community building. Reading different story lines in the same book provides students with a like text and provides them with ideas to discuss. They see that they can learn from one another as a result of reading and talking about the different story lines within the texts. They see themselves as capable. You may recall that we provide six reasons for using a variety of texts in the opening chapter. Here's how they apply to multilevel texts.

To Better Motivate All Readers

An examination of the multilevel texts shown on the list at the end of this chapter is sure to reveal one common characteristic: interesting content. And interest appears to be an excellent vehicle for motivating students to read. But beyond interesting content, another way that multilevel texts are enticing, especially for older students who struggle with reading, is that they let these students see themselves as one of the gang, if you will. After all, they can read the same text as another student that they might perceive as more capable. Instead of seeing themselves as readers who must read picture books while others are reading chapter books, they see that *all* readers are reading picture books.

To Shed Light on the Complexity of Reading

We rely on many different skills and strategies when we read different texts. In short, we employ different cognitive structures when we read different kinds of texts. For example, we first think of our purpose for reading the text. Is it for enjoyment? Are we trying to learn from the text? Determining our purpose for reading helps us approach the text in ways that enable us to achieve our goal. Multilevel texts highlight skills such as these in a very natural way. That is, readers set purposes relative to the story line they will be reading. When reading *Robots Slither!* (Hunter 2004), for instance, children who read the story line told in simple rhyming verse will most likely focus on the pleasure of hearing the language roll off their tongues. Those who focus on the nonfiction story line will read to learn specific information about different robots.

To Expand Children's Understandings of the Variety of Text Genres and Structures

We seem to do a pretty good job of exposing children to some genres, such as fiction, but not so well with others, such as nonfiction. Several researchers (e.g., Duke 2000) have discovered that nonfiction needs more attention in the primary grades so that children can be as comfortable with that text structure as they are with story grammar, the text structure authors use when writing stories. Instead of thinking that first children learn to read in the early elementary grades and then read to learn in the upper-elementary grades, we now see that children learn to read and read to learn at the same time and that this learning begins even before kindergarten as children notice and learn from their print-rich environment. Multilevel texts help us accomplish this most important goal because more often than not, authors use different genres for the different story lines in the text. We can call attention to one or both types of writing and teach children about the differences among them.

To Make More Texts Acceptable and Accessible in and out of School

The whole premise of this book is that we need to make as many texts as possible both acceptable and accessible. We make them acceptable by using them at school in a variety of ways, showing rather than telling students that reading many different kinds of texts is the hallmark of an excellent reader. We make them accessible by scaffolding instruction so that children experience reading success. Multilevel texts enable scaffolding. As a result of reading a given story line and listening to a more sophisticated story line from the same text, for example, children develop additional background and broaden their knowledge base. Consequently, they are more likely to revisit the text independently and feel comfortable attempting the more challenging story line. What's more, because of their positive previous experiences with the text, children are apt to read it again, providing themselves with meaningful rereading.

To Help Children Develop an Understanding of Intertextuality

When we think of intertextuality, we often think in terms of different texts relating to different texts. One ingenious feature about multilevel books is that the intertextuality exists within a single text. Take *Built to Last* (Sullivan

2005), for example. Within this one text, readers can gain information about a given bridge, dam, tunnel, or skyscraper in one of three ways: First, they can simply read the label and look at the picture. Second, they can take a look at the brief information at the bottom of the page. Third, they can read the narrative written to tell more about the given bridge, dam, tunnel, or skyscraper. Then, too, they can look at the additional information included in the color-coded sidebars that appear sporadically throughout the text. Combining all of these sources, then, provides students with a greater understanding about how all of these different texts can work together.

To Address the Oversimplification of Leveling Systems Often Used to Determine Which Books Children Should Read

"Good grief!" you might be thinking to yourself. "How can we put multi-level texts in our book room? Which level do we use?" And this is exactly one of our points. While leveling books can be advantageous, it can also cause problems for teachers and children alike. For example, as a result of using specific criteria to level books (see Peterson 1991), we begin to think of books as levels, often forgetting that as important as book level is the child and teacher interaction that accompanies the book (Clay 1991). If we believe in the idea that readers bring meaning to the printed word and that they interact with the author to construct meaning, then we have to take differing backgrounds into consideration when determining levels. In other words, while a book may be assigned to a given level, a child may or may not be able to read it based on background experiences.

Multilevel texts, then, help us remember that books can represent more than one level. They shake up the book-leveling paradigm, reminding us to think about other reading-related factors (see Chapter 1). As a result of using the same text with many different children, we can differentiate instruction and also convey to students that some texts provide common understandings that are good for all.

"But we have to level!" you say? Every problem has a solution. You can level each story line within the text. You can identify the story and its corresponding level on the back of the book, similar to the way you code other texts. You might even have a special place in your bookroom titled "Multi-level Texts."

How Might They Be Used?

Read-aloud: Perhaps one of the best ways to expose children to different text structures is by reading different types of texts aloud. Doing so implants the structure in their minds, enabling them to feel more at ease when encountering different texts on their own. In other words, the read-aloud enables learners to focus on listening comprehension as a segue to reading comprehension. Using multilevel books that contain different genres enables you to help children see the differences of text structures if you choose to read more than one story line. You might also choose to focus on the story line that contains the text structure you are trying to help implant in children's minds.

Shared reading: During shared reading, students are invited to read along when they can. Multilevel texts offer a sure fit for this strategy. Take *Robots Slither!* (Hunter 2004), for example. The simple rhyming text offers much information about robots. After you read the book aloud for enjoyment, children can then join in a second or third reading of the book. But there's an added bonus to using a multilevel book such as this for shared reading. That is, in the case of *Robots Slither!* because the author provides another story line that tells about the specific robot told in the rhyme, you can read aloud this text after children have read the whole rhyming story or you can have students pause after reading a given line so that you can insert the second story line, which provides additional information about the robot.

Guided reading: In *Reaching Readers* (Opitz and Ford 2001), we offer some specific suggestions for how to use multilevel texts for guided reading. These suggestions still ring true:

1. If you group students by similar level or background, different groups can read different parts of the text. For example, when reading multilevel texts such as *Sharks and Other Dangers of the Deep* (Mugford 2005), those who are just getting a handle on how print functions can read the names of the ocean creatures with the help of the supportive pictures and your assistance as needed. If these students have little background information about the text, you can have them follow along as you read, and on a second read, have them read with you. You can then read the other story line, which provides additional information about each ocean creature. Doing so broadens students' background and knowledge base.

2. Once each group member reads through the text, focusing on the most appropriate story line for the given group (i.e., similar achievement), children in different groups can be regrouped by twos (if the text has two story lines) or threes (if the book has three story lines). In turn, each person can read his or her part of the text while the

others listen. The result? Children, regardless of reading level, learn from one another.

Independent reading: As with other print material, multilevel texts can be an integral part of the classroom library and students can self-select them for independent reading. True, as Allington (2006) notes, children need to read, read, read, and they need books that they can read. And this is exactly what multilevel texts can provide. Children can determine which parts they are most comfortable reading; they need not read all story lines. Likewise, more children can read fewer books. That is, because multilevel books contain more than one story line, each written at different levels of complexity, one title can provide a range of readers with appropriate independent reading experiences.

Using Multilevel Texts with Younger Elementary-Aged Readers

Teaching second grade for the last three years has helped Jonathan realize that regardless of the class, most children seem interested in learning about dinosaurs. In fact, when brainstorming with students about dinosaurs, he discovered that they already know quite a bit about them.

Teaching second grade has also helped Jonathan to see that he must differentiate his instruction in order to reach as many learners as possible. It seems as though he always has a few students who are just learning to read, some who read fairly well, and some who can read just about anything he shows them. Recognizing these differences yet also wanting to unify his class, he decides to use a multilevel text during a shared reading experience. He selects *Dinosaur Picture Pops* (Tainish and Mugford 2004a). He will invite students to read the large print that names the dinosaur that pops up on each page. He will then read the additional information about that dinosaur to the class. He gathers his students together and proceeds.

"Yesterday we made a long list of what you already know about dinosaurs. I found a new book that I think you'll like. We might be able to add some information to our class list after we get finished reading it. What I need you to do is to read the name of the dinosaur that pops up when I open the page. After you read the name of the dinosaur, I will read the other information that tells more about it." They read the book. As students say the name of the dinosaur, Jonathan points to the corresponding text and shows them how to use the pronunciation guide below the word. Once finished, they return to each page to determine if there is any information they can add to their chart.

Finally, Jonathan points out that there are other dinosaurs named and explained on each page and that he will put the book in the classroom library for independent reading time. He encourages students to use what they learned about using the pronunciation guide below each word to help them pronounce names of the other dinosaurs shown in the text.

Using Multilevel Texts with Older Elementary-Aged Readers

Sheryl wants her fourth graders to study the United States, and she has selected *The Train of the States* (Sis 2004), a multilevel text, to help her do just that. She feels that this type of text will enable her to build community in her classroom while at the same time provide students of varying reading levels some appropriate-level text. Her observations of student and their performance on reading-related tasks have shown her that she has quite a spread of reading levels in her class.

To make the reading of the different story lines more manageable, Sheryl groups her students by their ability. Some of the children will read to discover the name of the state, the year of statehood, and who the state was named for. Other children will read to discover the name of the capital and the state flower, tree, and bird. Still other students will read to discover the fun fact about each state.

To prepare for the reading, Sheryl secures four copies of the text. She also decides to create a large blank map of the United States for all to see. As different groups of students read and discover specific information about the given state, she will invite them to add this information to the map. In this way, all students will contribute to the class map of the United States.

Sheryl also notices that there is additional information about each state in the back of the text. She will use the additional text at the end of the book to pique students' interest in each state. She will read it to students throughout their study of the United States.

Preparations in order, Sheryl calls the whole class together and explains the procedure, saying something like this: "Today we are going to begin learning more about the United States. You have already told me some facts you know about each state and we are going to add to them. Here's how we are going to do this." She continues by showing students a copy of the book and says, "When you come to read with me, you will all be reading the same book, but you will be reading different parts of it. You will also be adding important information to our classroom map. By the time you are finished reading, you will know a lot about the United States and you will have helped one another to learn."

Over the next few days, Sheryl has the different groups read the appropriate parts of the text so that they learn how to be better readers and feel successful. She also has each group add information to particular states on the map. At the end of the day, Sheryl calls the whole class together, reviews the map with them, and reads some additional information from the back of the book.

Sample Titles

Books with Two Story Lines

Title	Author	Genre(s)	Company/Year ISBN	Suggested Grade Levels*
Big Bugs! Giant Creepy Crawly Pop-Ups	Faulkner	• Nonfiction	Scholastic/2003 0439499054	1–2
Dinosaur Picture Pops	Tainish and Mugford	• Nonfiction	St. Martin's/ 2004 0312493436	1–2
Dog's A B C: A Silly Story About the Alphabet	Dodd	• Nonfiction • Fiction • Includes summary	Dutton/2000 052546837	1–2
Jungle	Tainish and Mugford	• Nonfiction	St. Martin's/2004 0312494491	1–2
Machines	Tainish and Mugford	• Nonfiction	St. Martin's/2004 0312494661	1–2
Alpha, Bravo, Charlie: The Military Alphabet	Demarest	• Nonfiction • Author's note at end	McElderry/2005 0689869282	1–3
Beaks!	Collard III	• Nonfiction • Summary page to review	Charlesbridge/ 2002 1570913889	1–3
Elephants Can Paint, Too!	Arnold	• Fiction • Nonfiction	Simon and Schuster/2005 068986985	1–3

Title	Author	Genre(s)	Company/Year ISBN	Suggested Grade Levels*
A Platypus, Probably	Collard III	• Nonfiction	Charlesbridge/ 2005 1570915849	1–3
Sharks	Mugford	• Nonfiction	St. Martin's/2005 0312495331	1–3
Ocean Counting	Pallotta	• Nonfiction • Fiction	Charlesbridge/ 2005 0881061506	1–4
Robots Slither!	Hunter	• Fiction • Nonfiction • Concludes with additional information	Putnam/2004 0399237747	1–4
Grandma Elephant's in Charge	Jenkins	• Fiction • Nonfiction • Concludes with additional information and index	Candlewick/2003 0763620742	2–3
Faces in the Forest	Hirschi	• Nonfiction • Concludes with additional information	Penguin/1997 0525652248	2–4
Ice Bear: In the Steps of the Polar Bear	Davies	• Fiction • Nonfiction • Includes index	Candlewick/2005 0763627593	2–4
The Queen's Progress: An Elizabethan Alphabet	Mannis	• Historical fiction • Nonfiction • Concludes with additional information about queen	Penguin/2003 0670036129	3–5
Wise Guy: The Life and Philosophy of Socrates	Usher	• Fiction • Nonfiction • Concludes with additional information	Farrar, Straus, Giroux/2005 0374312494	3–6
One Leaf Rides the Wind	Mannis	• Poetry • Nonfiction	Penguin/2002 0670035254	4–5

*Grade at which several children should be able to read the easiest part of the text; grade at which most students will be interested in the text's content.

Books with Three Story Lines

Title	Author	Genre(s)	Company/Year ISBN	Suggested Grade Levels*
One Child, One Seed: A South African Counting Book	Cave	• Fiction • Nonfiction • Includes additional information	Holt/2002 0805072047	1–2
New York, New York: The Big Apple from A to Z	Melmed	• Fiction • Nonfiction • Includes tidbits about each place throughout illustrations • Includes summary	HarperCollins/2005 0060548762	3–5
The Train of the States	Sis	• Nonfiction • Concludes with additional information about illustrations	Greenwillow/2004 0060578394	3–5
Built to Last: Building America's Amazing Bridges, Dams, Tunnels, and Skyscrapers	Sullivan	• Nonfiction • Includes table of contents, references, and index	Scholastic/2005 0439517370	4–6

*Grade at which several children should be able to read the easiest part of the text; grade at which most students will be interested in the text's content.

Conclusions

Multilevel texts help build a community of learners while also attending to learners' unique needs. Because the texts contain two or more story lines written at various degrees of difficulty, they enable us to provide differentiated instruction with relative ease. They are yet another type of text that provides rich, interesting content written in different genres, exposing children to different types of text structures. They provide opportunities for meaningful rereading and can serve as scaffolds, enabling students to read beyond their perceived reading levels. Finally, multilevel texts are cost-effective. Because more children of varying levels can engage with a given title, you can purchase more titles that will reach a larger audience and stay within your current budget.

CHAPTER 5

Newspapers

Much has been said and written on the utility of newspapers; but one principal advantage which might be derived from these publications has been neglected; we mean that of reading them in schools, and by the children in families.

—Editorial from the *Eastern Herald* (Portland, Maine), 1795

A Brief Description

Think of newspapers as anthologies, because they are in their own way, aren't they? Like anthologies, newspapers are collections of writing. It just so happens that unlike most anthologies, newspapers bring together a variety of writing: articles, advertisements (full page, half page, classified), comic strips, editorials, letters to the editor, picture essays—quite a collection, indeed. The majority of this collection is written to inform the general public of current daily happenings (thus, the daily paper). And regardless of where the newspapers are published, all share one common characteristic: flimsy paper that's hard to handle out of doors should there be even the slightest breeze.

Beyond the daily newspaper, there are newspapers such as the *Weekly Reader* designed for classroom use. Several daily papers also insert a mini-newspaper, sometimes called the minipage, once each week.

Why Use Them?

Do high test scores mean anything to you in this age of high-stakes testing and accountability? If so, you will definitely want to use newspapers—at least based on what we've been reading lately. Some researchers are reporting that students who use newspapers as one print source along with their course textbooks have better achievement scores in social studies, language arts, and mathematics (Shapley 2001; Palmer, Fletcher, and Shapley 1994). Another researcher reports that according to the results of his longitudinal study, which followed three hundred children through first and second grades, children who regularly read the newspaper outperformed their peers by more than two grade levels, according to their performance on a reading achievement test (Edfeldt 1990).

Not interested in test scores? Then consider a more practical reason for using newspapers: they're cheap! It can be as simple as picking up the paper off your very own driveway and bringing it to class. Do this for a week and you'll have quite a bit of reading material. But if you would rather keep your paper at home, you can also get a classroom subscription that will yield one copy per day. This might be enough depending on how you intend to have students engage with the newspaper. If you need more copies of a single issue, Newspapers in Education (NIE), which has been around since 1930, when the *New York Times* designed one of the first newspapers-in-education programs, just might be for you. Visit www.naafoundation.org for a wealth of information about NIE, including extensive manuals you can use to better understand the program and how to get started. Need additional ideas for funding? Go to www.pantagraph.com/education/nie/#goals for information about how Pantagraph in central Illinois partners up with corporate sponsors who provide monies for the newspapers.

Add to these reasons the following six, which were first introduced in Chapter 1, and you're sure to be convinced, or to be able to convince skeptics, of the value of using newspapers.

To Better Motivate All Readers

Just last night Michael Opitz was talking with a friend about this writing project. When he told the friend that he was writing a chapter on using newspapers in school as one type of text to teach reading, the friend related this story about his older brother: "I mean, they tried everything to get the kid to read. They were readers themselves and had many kinds of reading material in the house such as books, newspapers, and magazines. They were excellent role models as they read their books and other print material in the evening after dinner and we were encouraged to do the same once homework was completed. But nothing seemed to work until my mother noticed something. My brother seemed glued to the classified ads in the newspaper. She started to notice that he would read the ads while the rest of us were reading books or magazines or other parts of the paper. To this day, she swears that the classified ads are what made him a reader. He still reads few books, but you should see the guy! He spends hours of time on eBay, buying and selling all sorts of stuff. He has to be a reader in order to get the best buys."

We share this story as a reminder that children come to reading through different texts, including newspapers. We have the potential to reach more readers when we use texts that will motivate them to engage with reading. Engagement is critical. As Braunger and Lewis (2006) note as a result of their literature review, one core understanding about how children develop as readers is that they must read and read often. How fortunate that this boy had parents who saw that the classified ads served to motivate their son's reading and let him read what interested him as a segue into the reading process itself. They showed him that they valued the classified ads as much as other print material, enabling their son to experience the pleasure of reading.

To Shed Light on the Complexity of Reading

Sorting pictures, advertisements, articles related to a specific topic—all of these are activities students can complete with the newspaper, and we suppose there is some value in them in that they do teach students something about classifying. But reading is so much more complex! When we think of using the newspaper to teach students something about reading, we think of going beyond surface-level activities such as these. For example, having students sequence comic strips is one activity we discovered as we were researching what others have to say about teaching with newspapers. But why have students sequence comic strips? Indeed, why teach sequencing at all? How does this skill relate to reading? In other words, how does knowing about sequencing enable better reading? Taking sequencing a step further would help students better understand the relationship of sequencing to reading. For example, a teacher can talk with students about how authors sequence their ideas so that readers can better comprehend the entire story. She can share with them the importance of organization as a vehicle for both writing and reading a comprehensible story. This is as true for comic strips as it is for written stories. She might decide to use comic strips as a first step in helping students understand this most important idea and proceed to using an article from the newspaper to extend the understanding of sequencing to narrative text. The point is to go beyond the surface to help students develop a deeper understanding of sequencing.

To Expand Children's Understandings of the Variety of Text Genres and Structures

Newspapers are filled with different types of text structures. While we might use *stories* as a general term to refer to articles, there are different types of articles. For example, some report hard news, in which little more than specific facts are given. Other stories such as editorials rely much on opinion. Still other articles are news analysis stories written to help readers form a judgment. So within this one story genre, there are different types of stories. Yet other forms of text structure appear in the newspaper, including tables, graphs, and diagrams. Using the newspaper, then, can familiarize students with these many different forms of writing, therefore enabling them to better comprehend different forms of writing (Shapely 2001).

To Make More Texts Acceptable and Accessible in and out of School

Perhaps one of the main reasons for using the newspaper is that it provides much reading material that pertains to the everyday lives of students. In a sense, it validates their worlds; they can relate to many of the reported events. But it can also add to their knowledge base if they rarely read the newspaper or listen to the news at home. Using the newspaper in school shows children that we accept it as one type of valuable text. And they also feel a certain amount of pride in recognizing that they can read something that others in their community read nearly every day.

Our own teaching experiences help us see that we sometimes take much for granted. For example, because we can afford to have a subscription to the newspaper, we are tempted to assume that all or most of our students' parents can do the same. It's only when we come to know students and their families that we are reminded that our assumption is not always correct. Some students have little or no access to a newspaper. All the more reason, then, for using newspapers in the classroom. It makes them accessible to students who would otherwise not have access.

To Help Children Develop an Understanding of Intertextuality

The thought occurred to us as we wrote this chapter that there are parts of the newspaper that are similar to other texts. For example, most newspapers have an index, as do the majority of textbooks. When we use the newspaper to help students develop an understanding of an index and how it can enable them to be more efficient readers, we can also help them make the connection with their textbooks, which are often more difficult to navigate. In other words, we can use the newspaper as a springboard into more difficult texts. In addition to becoming more efficient readers, students also begin to further develop the notion of intertextuality, the idea that some texts share common characteristics.

To Address the Oversimplification of Leveling Systems Often Used to Determine Which Books Children Should Read

No question about it. There are many different text levels within any given newspaper. The classified advertisements are less complex than a full-length article. Some articles are more complex than others. Even different comic strips are written at different levels of complexity. One of the benefits of using newspapers, then, is that regardless of perceived or assessed reading level, all students are sure to find some part that they are able to read.

How Might They Be Used?

Read-aloud: One of the benefits of reading aloud to students is that it emphasizes listening comprehension, a skill that needs to be taught more often than not (see Opitz and Zbaracki 2005 for a review of supportive studies). Students need not concern themselves with decoding because they are listening rather than reading. This means that through listening, they can comprehend material that they might not otherwise manage. The newspaper offers numerous opportunities for read-alouds. You can give students a purpose for listening before reading a given article, such as to see if they can figure out what a given word means, or if they can identify the order in which an event happened, or if they can identify three facts the author states in the article. Purpose established, you proceed to read the selected article and, once finished, provide time for student responses related to the stated purpose for listening.

Not to be missed in several newspapers is the serialized story, in which individual chapter(s) are provided over a period of time. Usually, one chapter is included each week. These stories are superb read-aloud material because they are authentic texts that appeal to elementary-aged students. You can also use these stories as a means of helping students learn how to retell a story. Before reading this week's chapter, you can begin by asking children, "Now where did we leave off? What did we predict that might happen in the next chapter?" You might even have an evolving chart on which you record student comments from week to week.

Shared reading: Remember that during shared reading, students are invited to read along as they can. True, as teachers, we most often have a teaching point in mind such as teaching beginning readers left-to-right progression or speech-to-print matching. Nevertheless, having students read with us is a part of the shared reading experience. With some modifications, newspapers are viable texts for accomplishing purposes such as these. For example, we can select specific articles and display them for all to see. Pointing to the large print, we can read the title of an article and invite students to share what they think it will be about. In this case, we need not concern ourselves with reading the small print that accompanies each article. We can summarize it for the students and proceed to the next selected article and repeat the process.

Guided reading: Newspapers and small-group guided reading are a good fit. Remember that one reason we call students together to guide their reading is to teach them more about the reading process. We might want to teach them about how to make inferences or how to visualize when reading text. We can teach strategies such as these with many different texts, newspapers included. And what a great way to use the classic *Weekly Reader* that graces most elementary school classrooms. Instead of the all too familiar whole-group round-robin reading prompted by statements such as "Let's take a look at our *Weekly Reader* that arrived today. Please read the first part on the first page, John. The rest of you please follow along," we can use the text during small-group guided reading to teach a specific reading strategy. In this way we can get more mileage out of the *Weekly Reader* because more students have to read more of the text (instead of following along—or pretending to do so—as others read aloud). We can also plan to use the *Weekly Reader* as a way to differentiate instruction with relative ease. Using the same issue, we can teach different children different reading strategies. Some children, for example, might need additional practice with rereading to verify a response. Others might need to practice reading with fluency. Still others might need additional help in understanding how to summarize.

Independent reading: Independent reading is one of the major reasons for including newspapers in your classroom. Several students such as those with the second profile ("I don't like reading!") and the third profile ("I'm not very good at reading."), as discussed in Figure 1.1, are likely to find the newspaper enticing. Instead of having to focus on text that primarily contains one story, they can look at several different kinds of writing. They might look at the classified ads or the comic strips. They might choose to look at photographs and the captions that accompany them. By having newspapers available during independent reading, we send a message to students that newspapers are valuable reading sources. Likewise, we permit students to read the parts that they want to read. Student choice is an excellent way to build ownership with the selected text and a desire to read it (Turner 1995). And, yes, we are also indirectly teaching them to read selectively (i.e., to make decisions about what they want to read, skip, skim, or reread). Reading selectively is but one reading strategy that better ensures students learn from text (Duke and Pearson 2002).

Using Newspapers with Younger Elementary-Aged Readers

Josh wants his third graders to learn about how an index can save them time when reading the newspaper or any text that has an index, for that matter. He gathers the students in their meeting area and begins his whole-class lesson: "Today I want to show you something that will save you a lot of time when reading to locate specific information. It's called an index." He points to the front page of the local paper, which he brought to class for this very purpose.

He continues, "As you can see, this index shows you what's in the paper, the major parts or sections of the paper. Let's say you want to go to a movie but you aren't sure what's showing or the show times. Rather than go through every section of the newspaper, you can look at the index to find which section of the newspaper will show you." He points to the text as he says, "Notice that this index actually uses the word *movies* and that you will find information in the A section on page 7." He then turns to page 7 of the A section to show students that the index does, indeed, take them to the correct page to find the needed information.

Josh continues the lesson by giving students additional practice with the index. He poses statements such as, "You want to find out who won the high school football game. Take a look at the index to see which section you need to find and the page or pages that might provide that information." He provides time for student responses and also calls on a volunteer to cross-check with the newspaper by turning to the appropriate page.

Josh closes the lesson by stating, "Using an index can save you a lot of time. Instead of having to look at every page, you can go right to the section that has the information you want to discover."

Using Newspapers with Older Elementary-Aged Readers

Valarie knows that her fifth-grade students have been exposed to identifying fact and opinion, but she's not convinced that many students know how this knowledge applies to their reading. She sees the newspaper as an excellent way to better ensure that students develop this understanding while teaching something about the newspaper at the same time. She will use fact and opinion to show students how an editorial (which relies on opinions) is different from a news story (which relies on facts).

She begins the lesson by providing students with a list of facts, which she places on an overhead transparency. She asks students to read the statements and to note what they have in common. Different students volunteer that all of the statements are statements that can be proved to be true. "You are correct," Valarie comments, "and we usually call these *facts.*" She follows the same process with opinions and, based on student responses, concludes that the students understand the basic difference between the two. She shares her conclusion with the class. "It looks to me like you have a good handle on how facts and opinions are different. But what I want to know is how does knowing this help you read a text such as a newspaper?" Some students volunteer that knowing the difference will help them to determine how much they should believe when reading a given article. Valarie responds, "That's correct. And there are different parts of the newspaper that are basically an opinion and others that are based on fact. Knowing these differences will help you make an informed decision about what you've read—how much you should believe and if you need further information to verify what the author is stating. Let's see if you can discover which of these pieces of writing is based on opinion and which is based on fact."

In turn, she displays an overhead transparency showing an editorial and one with a news article and provides students with time to read each. She then displays the individual articles and provides students with time to state either facts or opinions noted in each. As they volunteer comments, she underlines the facts or opinions they point out. Finally, she shares with students that the article based on an opinion is called an editorial, whereas the one based on fact is called a news story. She concludes by saying, "When you are reading the different parts of the newspaper, such as these two types of articles, you have to think about what the author is trying to share with you and whether or not it is based on opinion or fact. Doing so helps you to be a critical reader; it helps you think for yourself, which is a big part of reading."

Sample Titles

local newspaper(s) (all grades, depending on how they are used)
Weekly Reader (preschool–grade 6)
kids page or minipage from local newspaper (grades 1–3)
Scholastic News (grades 1–6)

Four Additional Considerations

1. Remember that some students may have never fully experienced reading the newspaper. You will need to show them what it means to read the paper as opposed to how they might read other texts to alleviate any concerns about reading the vast amount of pages word for word. They need to develop the understanding that very seldom do readers read every single article and section of the newspaper. Nonetheless, when asked if they have read the paper, most readers will say they have, meaning that they have read the sections and articles that mattered to them.

2. Provide students with an overview of the newspaper so that they can get an overall sense of how the paper is structured. They can then focus on individual sections of interest.

3. Consider how much of the newspaper you want students to have at any one time. When teaching kindergarten, Michael Opitz made the mistake of giving children too much at once. While their lack of success might have appeared to be student centered, it was anything but that. It was a teacher-centered problem. The next time he had them use the newspaper to identify words they knew, he gave each of them one quarter of one page. They were all successful.

4. Think about having your students create their own newspaper. Yes, we know that the idea of creating a classroom newspaper is anything

but revolutionary; however, the lesson plan that Laurie Henry shares online, titled "Creating a Classroom Newspaper," certainly is! She breathes new life into creating classroom newspapers by offering ten fifty-minute lessons geared toward helping students in grades 3 through 5 create an authentic newspaper. In addition to the lessons, she also shares specific objectives, content standards, and additional resources. The best news is that it is all free. Simply go to www.readwritethink.org/lessons, click on "3–5" on the grade band, and look for the specific lesson title.

Conclusions

We agree with Backes, who states, "One of the oldest of living language activities, almost as old as printing itself is the newspaper. . . . Every school should have one" (1995, 17). To this we would add that every school should have more than one! Newspapers are easily accessible but they also need to be acceptable in classrooms. Newspapers are equitable with other texts, as the many reasons and suggestions for using newspapers in this chapter illustrate. Not only do they help round out the reading diet, but they can get some students to begin a reading diet, potentially providing them with nourishment and energy to tackle other texts.

Websites

We are not at a loss for websites related to using newspapers. Here are five of our top picks:

www.naafoundation.org provides a wealth of information about Newspapers in Education (NIE), including extensive workshop manuals and teaching ideas. It also provides a brief historical background of the organization.

www.readwritethink.org/lessons is a website created by the International Reading Association (IRA) and the National Council of Teachers of English (NCTE) that provides teacher-created lesson plans on several different topics. These lessons can serve as launching pads for creating your own plans and promise to be time-savers.

www.pantagraph.com/education/nie/#goals provides information about how an organization in central Illinois operates. It provides several

ideas for how to get newspapers into schools, information on funding
sources, and teaching ideas.

www.pjstar.com/services/nie/pages/middleteachers.html provides upper-
elementary and middle school teachers with several reasons and ideas
for using newspapers. It also provides a list of free curriculum materials for NIE participants.

www.press-enterprise.com/nie/tips_np_at_home.html offers several suggestions for using newspapers at home. Suggestions include reading
tips for parents and thirteen simple activity ideas.

6

Series Texts

When I was ten years old, I wrote: "I will be happy if I can have horses, solve mysteries, help people, and be happily married." In that order. For thirty years after that, I forgot on any conscious level about that wish list. When I finally came across it again, I was forty years old, married to a cowboy, doing volunteer work, and writing murder mysteries. . . . It's easy enough to figure out why I wanted to "have horses"—doesn't almost every adolescent girl dream of riding Black Beauty? Growing up in the fifties made it de rigueur for me to want to "be happily married," and being a college student in the sixties made it nearly obligatory for me to want to "help people." But whence the desire to "solve mysteries"? That's easy, isn't it? I read Nancy Drew. Didn't you?

—Nancy Pickard, *I Owe It All to Nancy Drew*

The odd thing was that the most bookish children I knew—precisely those who were recognized by their teachers as the best readers and writers— were usually the most avid readers of series books. Children simply discounted the advice of the librarians, bypassing libraries altogether to buy private collections of series books, which were energetically discussed, traded and saved. —Catherine Sheldrick Ross, "If They Read Nancy Drew, So What? Series Book Readers Talk Back"

A Brief Description

For this section, we will define *series texts* as a collection of texts containing multiple titles that often feature the same central characters and/or formulaic development of the genre. Often these collections are created by the same author or publisher and branded together by the name of the characters (e.g., Kids of Polk Street School) or the genre (Goosebumps). Some collections are limited series like a trilogy while others are quite extensive in the number of related titles they offer.

Why Use Them?

In her awarding-winning research, Catherine Ross (1995) has documented that almost as long as there have been series books there has also been a debate by adults about their value for children. She shares one debate that occurred in the late 1800s. On one hand, librarian Herbert Putnam argued against the use of series books, concluding that since libraries were an extension of the educational system, it was not their responsibility "to provide people with flabby mental nutriment" (263). On the other hand, another librarian, W. A. Bardwell, concluded: "[T]he reading of light works of fiction by boys is better than no reading and . . . its tendency is to cultivate a taste for literature that will, in turn, demand something better" (208). In her study, Ross observes that the adult disdain for series reading often is at odds with the positive value placed on series books by lifelong readers.

Series books have unique instructional and recreational features. These features may encourage significant self-initiated reading practice that can improve a reader's competence, confidence, and comfort. Key is the predictability of the formulaic features of each text. This makes it easier for readers to negotiate the language structures and content of each book. Students can develop literary competence by reading many different books in a familiar series. Rabinowitz (1987) argues that this repeated practice allows readers to pick up the "rules of reading" (43). Readers are more able to focus their attention on important textual features, creating a better framework for understanding the story. This may also be why some (Krashen 2004; Pilgren 2000) have pointed out the power of series reading for specific groups, like students who are English language learners (ELLs). Meek (1988) suggests that readers who read large quantities of texts they enjoy give themselves "private lessons" that cause them to learn many things about the reading process without ever being taught directly. In this section, let's look further at why adding the use of series books to a classroom reading program may help a teacher better address the many readers in that classroom.

To Better Motivate All Readers

Series reading may be critical for some key profiles defined in the motivation chart (Figure 1.1). Let's first look at the "I'm not very good at reading" students. As the motivation research reveals, readers who have the ability to read can cause problems for themselves just by thinking they are not very good readers. Self-efficacy is a critical affective dimension of successful readers. It leads to continued effort and risk taking. If someone sees herself as a good reader, she'll be more likely to continue to seek out what you have to teach her about being a better reader. Series reading may be able to positively affect a reader's view of himself as a reader. Series reading has a potential to build a reader's comfort level with reading. As he moves through titles, he can see his confidence rising and begin to convince himself that maybe he is a pretty good reader after all.

Series reading might also be good for those students who fit the "Reading is not very important to me" profile. These students often score quite high on the social dimension of the motivational scale. In fact, socializing often gets a higher priority and more attention than reading. We need to consider how to infuse reading instruction with greater social dimensions. Think about any time when you have discovered that you and a friend have been reading from the same series of books. Suddenly reading becomes the focus of the socializing. It sets up lots of opportunities to critically compare which books are better and why, make predictions about what might happen next, and share reactions to what is being read. Sometimes the fact that so many others are reading the series will produce the needed social pressure for some students to also pick up a book from the series. Reading certain series and genres actually takes on a bit of a subversive feel, strengthening their appeal to certain groups of students.

To Shed Light on the Complexity of Reading

Series books are formulaic. They have been compared to fast food (Ross 1995). They are a standardized commodity—readers know what they are getting. They are intentionally written with attention to consistent text, reader, and context factors. The text factors are built within predictable frames with recurring characters and features. While the content or concepts of the books will vary slightly, the format, organization, and author's purpose are consistent across texts. This allows the reader to draw on factors she brings to the page. While the introduction of a series needs as much attention as the introduction of any unfamiliar text, once students are familiar with a series, they need to do very little to ramp up for the start of a new title. Readers will already bring the background knowledge they need to the book. Their schema will be easily activated to facilitate comprehension. Very few new skills will be needed to handle the similarly crafted text of the new title after they are addressed in the introduction to the series. The reader can start with a self-directed purpose ("I need to find out what happens next") and with little need for external motivation. Series books are written to be read in a variety of settings, but the environment is usually psychologically safe and low risk. Series reading has a clear task and outcome for the reader. This consistency across contexts facilitates greater success with the reading of the series.

While some may question the degree of mental challenge that comes with the repeated practice of reading similar texts in a series, this practice can promote some key reading outcomes that transcend the series and lead to greater success with other reading experiences. For example, series reading can foster fluency. First the series sets up an opportunity for wide reading. This is often one of the best ways for readers to practice their skills and get better at them. Any reader moving through a series will get ample practice that should strengthen his fluency. A reader who has a strong sense of fluency will likely process texts more efficiently so that mental energy can be devoted to comprehension. Series reading allows the reader to get a sense of what fluent reading feels like and this will eventually transfer to texts outside the series. The reader more easily gets over the challenge of getting into the story and is less likely to give up too soon.

To Expand Children's Understandings of the Variety of Text Genres and Structures

Series reading tends to favor narrative story lines, but across a number of genres including realistic fiction, historical fiction, mystery, science fiction, and fantasy.

Some nonfiction historical accounts and biographies presented in series will also follow a narrative story line. This is not to say that other informational genres are not represented in series books, but these may be more often defined as reference material. What has been interesting to observe is the emergence of paired books in series—one story with one informational text. We see this in a series like the Magic Tree House. As we discussed in the chapter on multilevel books (see Chapter 4), sometimes we see information embedded in asides in series that have a narrative story line, like the Magic School Bus series.

Because narrative story lines dominate series books, these texts expose readers primarily to structures based on story grammar: characters (main and supporting), setting (time, place, and mood), goal(s), actions taken to achieve the goal(s), conflict(s), and resolution. Some of these story grammar elements like main characters and primary setting are consistent across the texts in the series. Other story grammar elements provide the variation among the texts. Because series books are formulaic, they are often more plot driven. Significant descriptive attention to characters and settings may be lacking. Most of the attention is given to creating the conflict and the steps toward resolution. While the texts are structured around story grammar, these books do lend themselves to work with compare-contrast and chronological structures. Teachers can work with compare-contrast graphic organizers using two books from a series to easily discuss how they are alike and different. The plot-driven nature of some series books also help readers learn to identify the sequence of events.

To Make More Texts Acceptable and Accessible in and out of School

Series books have had a long history of being devalued by the reading experts. Ross (1995) observes that throughout history, series books have been "anathemas" to librarians. "Librarians were very sure they knew exactly what was happening when a child read a series book, and none of it was good" (203). Teachers also have continually expressed their frustration with series books. The most common complaint usually relates to a student who will read only from that series and never has the same interest in reading other texts. Some series have a significant number of individual titles and/or are produced with great frequency, and some librarians and teachers envision the student never leaving the series. While we might be resolved to the fact that at least the student is reading, we begin to wonder how to introduce other books into this child's life. As someone once said, creating a habit is a good goal, but just because something is a habit doesn't necessarily mean it is good for you.

So why bring series books into the classroom reading program? Ross points out that no matter what experts think about series books, actual readers almost always paint a positive picture of their experiences with series reading. That may be the most obvious reason for bringing them into the classroom. Students will discover series books and will be reading them whether we allow them in the classroom or not. Most of us can remember a series that we devoured text after text—at least until we ran out of texts or discovered something new. Let's face it, series reading mirrors what many real readers do. Anyone who has worked in a bookstore knows that some of the most dependable customers are series readers. Customers rush to buy the latest titles in a genre series like Harlequin romances or science fiction titles in the Star Trek series. They often express displeasure when they know that they have to wait a bit longer for the latest title in a series they are eagerly awaiting (such as Sue Grafton's mystery novels). If series books are already playing a role in readers' lives and may play a role in any reader's life, capitalizing on that inherent interest is one reason for bringing the titles into the classroom.

That is not to say that concerns about series books are completely unwarranted. Some critics have pointed to racial, gender, and ethnic stereotypes in some series that end up being repeated over and over again as a reader moves from title to title. Others have noted the commercialization of some series to the degree that brand-name products are interspersed throughout the stories, making some series little more that advertisements. Still others have noted an increasing emphasis on sex and violence in series books as they try to compete with the content of other media. But even in those cases, where better to mediate a discussion about those issues than in the classroom with a teacher and peers?

To Help Children Develop an Understanding of Intertexuality

Series reading may be the first experience many students have that leads to the discovery that books do not need to stand alone. It is in reading books in a series that the reader realizes, "Hey, this book is connected to another one I read." Students begin to see that they can take what they have experienced in one book and use it to enjoy and understand another. Teachers can use series readings to introduce and foster intertextual connections. Once she has introduced her class to the first book in a series, the teacher can make a connection to another book in the series. After reading a second book, the teacher can encourage text-to-text connections, inviting students to talk about how the two books were alike and different. The problem with series reading is that the level of intertextual connections plateaus if the reader repeatedly reads texts from the same series. The reader needs to experience multiple series or texts outside the series to become capable of making more sophisticated connections among texts.

To Address the Oversimplification of Leveling Systems Often Used to Determine Which Books Children Should Read

Another nice feature of series books is that they exist at almost all reading levels. From simple chapter books, like Henry and Mudge, to complex titles consumed equally by children and adults, like Harry Potter, you should be able to find different series for children of diverse abilities in the same classroom. These series also often eliminate the need to consume valuable time trying to figure out the levels of individual titles. They are more formulaic and the individual titles in a series will probably be written at similar levels. Those trying to build a classroom collection of leveled texts may want to use series books. They are easily accessible. There are many titles readily available and often at relatively low cost. Series books are often abandoned once readers have moved on, so it is often easy to find used copies to add to a classroom library.

How Might They Be Used?

Series books have a potential role in all key components of a balanced literary program. Let's look at how the teacher can use them in a classroom reading program.

Read-aloud: Select a title from a collection of series books for read-aloud, usually as a way of introducing the series to your students. Once the title has been read aloud in the class, it is critical that the children have access to additional titles in the series. After introducing a series, however, move on to other titles outside of the series. Be intentional about using the read-aloud time to introduce other series, other titles by the author of the series, and/or other titles from the same genre of the series. The read-aloud time is a good time to jump-start reading habits, but once habits are started, the read-aloud time should be used to help children change courses with their reading habits. Because of the limited amount of time available for reading aloud, try to avoid repeated reading aloud from the same series.

Shared reading: Series books probably have only limited use as a vehicle for shared reading. If you are interested in introducing the series to jump-start reading habits, it might be better to use the read-aloud time to achieve that goal. If you are interested in using the series books as an instructional tool, it might be best to use multiple titles from the series in a guided reading group or as part of a focused workshop. If you are trying to foster a sense of community in the classroom, it might be best to introduce a series in the read-aloud and then encourage the reading of additional separate titles during independent reading time. While any selection from a series book could be use as part of a word identification or comprehension strategy demonstration in a large-group setting, you may want to be more intentional about selecting texts outside of a series to provide better models of quality writing for elementary students. One shared activity could be to use the books in a series as a catalyst for writing. Collectively analyze the formulaic structures of the books. Once readers have a good sense of how the books in a series are structured, you can introduce the structure as an organizer for planning the writing of a similar story that extends or innovates on the story elements at the heart of the series.

Guided reading: The formulaic nature of most series books makes them good instructional materials for guided reading instruction. The teacher can rest assured that the multiple titles in a series are approximately at the same level. When teachers lack multiple copies of the same text to use in small groups, more accessible multiple titles from a series might be a viable alternative. The teacher can assign everyone in a guided reading group a different title within the series. Instruction can be contextualized within the series, but conversations can occur across the texts. This sets up a natural bridge to independent reading. Titles shared during guided reading instruction can be traded with other group members for independent practice. If the readers trade multiple times, they will get practice with texts that are a bit familiar but still new to them. They will get to practice with different texts and not just the same text over and over again.

Independent reading: In her study, Ross (1995) discovered that many of the adult book readers she interviewed could identify a developmental phase of reading series books as a key in discovering the joy of independent reading. Sixty percent of these readers reported reading series books as children. In fact, series books, along with those that had been read aloud to them, were often the first books they remembered reading successfully on their own. So the best use of series books might be to foster independent reading.

First, series books can be a significant way to promote reading that is done away from the teacher, both in the classroom as well as beyond the classroom. Allowing access to these titles as part of a recreational reading program may be one way to capitalize on the natural gravitation toward these titles. Since these titles are so available, it might also be a great way for families to sustain the momentum of independent reading started in the school setting.

Second, if you are implementing a reading workshop approach as a part of your instructional program, the use of series books may be a good way to initially set up the classroom procedures for the workshop. Invite students to select any title from a specific series. Demonstrate how the workshop will work by developing focus lessons around the features of the series. Students can focus on applying those skills and strategies as they read in their titles from the series. Design response structures to take advantage of the features of the series as well. Students can use those structures to respond to the individual title they are reading. Meet with students to confer about their responses and facilitate a connected conversation across the individual titles of the series, or students can meet to share their responses with each other in a similar way. The workshop period can end with students sharing specific excerpts and responses from their individual titles and trying to see the connections and contrasts between the titles being read. As the students move through the series, you can use the time to introduce, develop, and practice the routines before opening up the workshop to include a greater diversity of titles and responses.

Using Series Texts with Younger Elementary-Aged Readers

It wouldn't have been Michael Ford's choice but when Jenny came in and asked him to read aloud her favorite book, it was hard to say no to the dog-eared copy of the first story in the Boxcar Children series. For the next few weeks, his first-grade class enjoyed listening to this mystery of the self-reliant siblings who have to hide the fact they are living without their parents in an abandoned railroad car. He decided to get just a little more mileage out of this read-aloud time. Since they were reading this mystery, he asked his students to listen each day for what they thought were the most important things that happened. At the end of the reading, Michael Ford grabbed a sheet of partially lined eighteen-by-fourteen-inch paper and quickly recorded what the children thought were the most important events in the story that day. Then he systematically assigned one child to add an illustration to each recorded summary to help them see what happened to the characters that day. Before starting a new chapter, they could review what had happened so far in the book by quickly looking at their illustrated summaries over the past few days. When they were done reading the book, they bound the summary pages together and created an abridged version of the book that all students could reread on their own time. Many students, however, were ready for additional unabridged versions of the Boxcar Children stories, and the book that Jenny brought for her teacher to read was the catalyst for many others to keep reading this series long after the class read-alouds were done.

Using Series Texts with Older Elementary-Aged Readers

Patti wanted to open up the choices in her fourth-grade classroom and move away from using the same text for all students. She was a bit cautious about making this change and decided the best way to introduce the idea of different students reading different books was to bring in a series. She began with the Encyclopedia Brown books, by Donald Sobol. With twenty-two titles available to choose from, she was able to find enough copies of different titles in this series to allow students to choose the title they wanted to read. Because everyone was reading from the same series, which was built on a mystery genre, she was able to create strategy lessons focused on reading for details, looking for clues, and making and checking predictions. She could maintain connected conversations across her classroom and still allow students some choice in the titles they were reading. This also fostered a community atmosphere in her classroom that led to students trading titles when they had finished with theirs. As Patti grew increasingly comfortable with opening up choice and using multiple titles during her reading classroom, she was able to differentiate even further by moving beyond the use of a single series of books.

Sample Titles

Series	Example Title	Author	Company/Year ISBN	Suggested Grade Levels
Junie B. Jones	*Junie B. Jones and the Mushy Gushy Valentine*	Park	Random House/ 1999 0375800345	pre-K–2
Magic Tree House	*Good Morning, Gorilla*	Pope Osborne	Random House/ 2002 0375806148	pre-K–2
Martha the Dog	*Martha the Talking Dog*	Medaugh	Merrymakers/ 2001 1579820328	pre-K–2
Henry and Mudge	*Henry and Mudge in Puddle Trouble*	Rylant	Aladdin/1996 0689810032	pre-K–3
Mercy Watson	*Mercy Watson to the Rescue*	DiCamillo	Candlewick/2005 0763622702	K–2
Mr. Putter and Tabby	*Mr. Putter and Tabby Write the Book*	Rylant	Harcourt/2005 015200241	K–2
Kids of Polk Street School	*Sunnyside Up*	Giff	Yearling/1986 0440484065	1–3
The Boxcar Children	*Surprise Island*	Chandler	Albert Whitman/ 1989 0807576743	2–4
Cam Jansen	*Cam Jansen and the Mystery of the Television Dog*	Adler	Scholastic/1981 0590461249	2–4

Series	Example Title	Author	Company/Year ISBN	Suggested Grade Levels
The Quigleys	*The Quigleys at Large*	Mason	David Fickling/ 2003 038575022	2–4
A to Z Mysteries	*The White Wolf*	Roy	Random House/ 2004 0375824804	3–5
Alien Adventures	*Aliens Ate My Homework*	Coville	Aladdin/1993 0671727125	3–5
Dive	*The Discovery*	Korman	Scholastic/2003 0439507227	3–5
Everest	*The Summit*	Korman	Scholastic/2002 0439411378	3–5
Internet Detectives	*Speed Surf*	Coleman	Skylark/1997 0553486225	3–5
The Lady Grace Mysteries	*Deception*	Burchett and Vogler	Delacorte/2005 0385733216	3–5
Mostly Ghostly	*Don't Close Your Eyes*	Stine	Delacorte/2006 0385746954	3–5
On the Run	*The Stowaway Solution*	Korman	Scholastic/2005 0439651395	3–5
Shiloh Trilogy	*Shiloh*	Reynolds Naylor	Aladdin/2000 0689835825	3–5
The Unicorn's Secret	*The Journey Home*	Duey	Aladdin/2003 0689853742	3–5
Wayside School	*Sideways Stories from Wayside School*	Sachar	HarperTrophy/ 2004 0380731487	3–5
Akiko	*The Training Master*	Crilley	Delacorte/2005 0385730438	3–6
The Boys	*A Traitor Among the Boys*	Reynolds Naylor	Random House/ 2001 0440413869	3–6
Captain Underpants	*Captain Underpants and the Attack of the Talking Toilets*	Pilkey	Scholastic/1999 0590634275	3–6
Chronicles of Narnia	*The Lion, the Witch and the Wardrobe*	Lewis	HarperTrophy/ 2000 0064409422	3–6
Flint Future Detectives	*Mr. Chickee's Funny Money*	Curtis	Wendy Lamb/ 2005 0385327722	3–6

Series	Example Title	Author	Company/Year ISBN	Suggested Grade Levels
The Girls	*A Spy Among the Girls*	Reynolds Naylor	Yearling/2002 0440413907	3–6
The Peppermints	*The Perils of Peppermint*	Brooks Wallace	Atheneum/2003 0689850433	3–6
The Plant That Ate	*The Plant That Ate Dirty Gym Socks*	MacArthur	Avon/1988 0380754932	3–6
Poppy Stories	*Poppy's Return*	Avi	HarperCollins/ 2005 0060000120	3–6
Sammy Keyes	*Sammy Keyes and the Dead Giveaway*	Van Draanen	Knopf/2004 0375823514	3–6
A Series of Unfortunate Events	*The Bad Beginning*	Snicket	HarperCollins/ 1999 0064407667	3–6
Shredderman	*Secret Identity*	Van Draanen	Knopf /2005 0375823514	3–6
The Edge Chronicles	*The Last of the Sky Pirates*	Stewart and Riddle	David Fickling/ 2002 038575018	4–6
Pure Dead	*Pure Dead Trouble*	Glori	Knopf/2005 0375833110	4–7
The Dragon Chronicles	*Dragon's Milk*	Fletcher	Aladdin/1997 0689716230	5–7
Eddie and the Gang with No Name	*Bring Me the Head of Oliver Plunkett*	Bateman	Delacorte/2005 0385902697	5–9
The Enchanted Forest Chronicles	*Dealing with Dragons*	Wrede	Jane Yolen/1990 0152229000	5–9
The Five Ancestors	*Monkey*	Stone	Random House/ 2005 0375830731	5–9
Harry Potter	*Harry Potter and the Half-Blood Prince*	Rowling	Scholastic/2005 0439784549	5–9
Wise Child Trilogy	*Wise Child*	Furlong	Random House/ 1989 0394825985	6–8
Hatchet	*Brian's Hunt*	Paulson	Wendy Lamb/ 2003 0385746474	6–9

Series	Example Title	Author	Company/Year ISBN	Suggested Grade Levels
Linus Hoppe	*The Destiny of Linus Hoppe*	Bandoux	Delacorte/2001 0385732295	6–9
The Sisterhood of the Traveling Pants	*The Second Summer of Sisterhood*	Brashares	Delacorte/2003 0385729340	6–9

Conclusions

Series texts will be a part of most readers' lives. To relegate them to second-class status in school reading programs seems foolish. They clearly are the best tool to address the motivational needs of some readers. The formulaic manner in which they are written allows the students a viable way to grow more comfortable, confident, and competent as readers. These books are readily available and lend themselves to use in achieving instructional goals related to fluency, narrative genres, story grammar text structures, and text-to-text connections. Series books are useful tools for linking read-alouds and guided reading to independent reading experiences. They are also a resource to consider when setting up guided reading and workshop experiences that allow students to read different texts but still be connected through conversations across those texts. While you may want to avoid overrelying on these materials, you certainly should consider how to use them intentionally and strategically to strengthen your classroom reading program.

Websites

General Website with Links to a Number of Series Books

www.kidsreads.com/series/index.asp, including
    The Boxcar Children: www.kidsreads.com/series/series-boxcar.asp
    Captain Underpants: www.kidsreads.com/series/series-capt.asp
    Encyclopedia Brown: www.kidsreads.com/series/series-brown.asp

Websites for Traditional Series

Nancy Drew: http://nancy-drew.mysterynet.com
The Hardy Boys: www.hardyboyscasefiles.com

Publisher's Website for The Magic Tree House

www.randomhouse.com/kids/magictreehouse

CHAPTER 7

Humorous Texts

Funniness runs in the human race. I mean books are written to make people laugh or for people to understand history and if half of the books written are to make people laugh we don't live forever so we can't read all the books so we just want to read the ones that are really funny.

—John, a fourth grader

One of the things I am most grateful to him [his father] for is that, contrary to educational principles, he allowed me to read comics. I think that is how I developed my love for English and for reading.

—Archbishop Desmond Tutu

A Brief Description

While working on his research in humorous children's literature, Matthew spent a lot of time pondering just what makes a text humorous. It's difficult for him to define the characteristics that make a text humorous, because in his mind *every* text that makes him smile or laugh is humorous. However, this is not the case with all readers. He's found that people react differently to what he perceives as humorous in different texts. He sees this time and again as he reads books aloud to different classes from elementary-aged children to college students. Some groups of students laugh hysterically at *Walter the Farting Dog* (Kotzwinkle and Murray 2001) while others are offended by such bathroom humor. Still others find Tacky the Penguin (e.g.,

95

Lester 1988, 2005) wild and crazy while others find him silly. Humor in texts is somewhat subjective, but texts that contain humor are still very appealing to many readers.

While Matthew's earlier research primarily focused on humorous children's literature selections, we go beyond children's literature when discussing the value of humorous texts in this chapter. For the purpose of this chapter, we define humorous texts as those written by authors with the sole purpose of making the reader laugh. They include picture books, chapter books, comic books, cartoons, and joke and riddle books.

Why Use Them?

A couple of years ago, Matthew designed and conducted a study to explore this question: Why should teachers use humorous texts in class? Using several different humorous children's literature titles, he studied how third- through fifth-grade students read, discussed, and engaged with the books. He found two primary reasons for using humorous books. The first reason is engagement. That is, he discovered that humorous books helped readers stay engaged with their reading. He also discovered that humorous books helped students with specific reading strategies such as visualization. In fact, the students he worked with described how funny books helped them with visualization, vocalization, and critical reading (Zbaracki 2003).

Finally, Matthew discovered that humorous books serve to motivate students' reading. Humorous books made his students want to read a lot as well as to "find the funny." Students were also motivated to share what they were reading with their classmates and friends (Zbaracki 2003).

Beyond Matthew's research, though, let's take a look at how humorous texts can help students with reading in terms of the reasons cited in Chapter 1.

To Better Motivate All Readers

Humorous texts can motivate all readers. However, in terms of the different reader profiles discussed in Figure 1.1, humor books definitely help motivate the first two groups: "I hate reading" and "I don't like reading!" Take "Donnie," a self-proclaimed reluctant reader, for example. He stated, "Reading is not my favorite thing" (Zbaracki 2003, 82). However, when reading humorous children's literature, his only struggle was deciding which book was going to be the last book he read for Matthew's study. Because of a limited amount of time, he could read only three of the selected five books. This "reluctant" reader had been drawn into the humorous books they had been reading.

The motivation to read humorous texts can become contagious and spread throughout a class or even several classes within a school when children read and share them. How often have you read or heard something funny, and your immediate response was to share the funny item with someone? This same phenomenon happens with children as they read humorous texts. There is a need to share what they have read. It might be with a classmate during class, with a friend on the bus, or even with a family member, but readers have a desire to share the funny moments with others (Zbaracki 2003). Encouraging students to read this genre and allowing these sharing moments help spread the intrinsic motivation to read.

To Shed Light on the Complexity of Reading

As mentioned in Chapter 1, reading is a complex behavior. Being able to use a variety of reading strategies such as visualization and having the ability to critically read are but two dimensions of this complexity. Humorous texts can help children learn many skills and strategies associated with reading. For example, one of Matthew's favorite characters in children's literature is Tacky the Penguin. He loves the visual of a penguin dressed in a Hawaiian shirt and wearing a bow tie. The crazy image that he creates in his mind is what makes Tacky so funny to him. In order for that to happen, however, he needs to use visualization, which humorous texts enable readers to do with relative ease. In other words, because authors and illustrators of humorous texts use words and illustrations in specific ways, both facilitate visualization.

Reading with expression is another reading skill that humorous texts facilitate. So many times the way characters speak or what they are saying makes the scene, or text, funny. Many readers tacitly understand this and often try on new and fun voices while they are reading. Readers understand that reading passages in a monotonous voice will not add to the fun and hilarity of the scene or text.

Critical reading (i.e., the ability to think reflectively and the ability to evaluate what to believe [Gunning 2003]) is another result of engaging with humorous texts. In other words, authors of humorous texts play with language in a very complex manner, as Norton Juster's *The Phantom Tollbooth* (1961) illustrates. Here's a sample passage:

"I thought you were the Weather Man," said Milo, very confused.

"Oh no," said the little man, "I'm the Whether Man, not the Weather Man, for after all it's important to know whether there will be weather than what the weather will be." (19)

In order to find this passage funny, or to get a joke or riddle, the reader must be able to understand double or even triple meanings of words, in this case the two different spellings and meanings of *weather* and *whether*. The reader must pay close attention to the written text and examine it critically for the understanding of homophones.

To Expand Children's Understandings of the Variety of Text Genres and Structures

Written humor comes in a variety of formats and authors use different text structures to write these different formats. Cartoons, picture books, comic books, and novels are types of humorous texts that can surround children. Children may start out reading humorous picture books such as *Tacky the Penguin* (Lester 1988), *Don't Let the Pigeon Drive the Bus* (Willems 2003), and *Arnie the Doughnut* (Keller 2003), which helps them further understand narrative story structure. Moreover, because the author of *Arnie the Doughnut* also employs cartoons, readers also get a sense of the structure that authors use to write cartoons. Likewise, Willems uses sequence boxes in *Don't Let the Pigeon Drive the Bus*, as do David Shannon in *Good Boy, Fergus!* (2006) and Sara Varon in *Chicken and Cat* (2006). Thus, when children attempt to read cartoons in other contexts, they'll have already been exposed to the cartoon structure and will be better able to comprehend the cartoon. The same can be said for comic books, which present a series of cartoons in sequence to tell a story.

Remember, too, that comic books and cartoon anthologies can be quite complex. They tell stories over a period of time, just as picture books and novels do. As Cary states, "Some titles contain complete, one-shot stories, many others feature 'continuity plots' that unfold—and typically cliffhang—issue to issue" (2004, 11). However, in comic book anthologies, readers have the option of looking back at previous strips to help remind them of the story line. Matthew is not ashamed to admit that he was disappointed when the creators of *Bloom County*, *The Far Side*, and *Calvin and Hobbes* all decided to end their strips. However, he was delighted to discover the anthologies of strips that they compiled and published. These anthologies allowed him the opportunity to rediscover the different stories in one book. He still pulls these books out and rereads them numerous times.

Comic books, cartoons, picture books, humorous novels, and, yes, even Captain Underpants have great value for readers. Including humorous texts in the class library signals acceptance of them to students. Inclusion of these titles also makes them more accessible for more students—that is, if you can keep them on the shelves! Just the other day, for example, Matthew was speaking with some teachers about graphic novels, which are similar to comic books. The main difference is they are bound in hardcover. These teachers had one common comment: More students than not enjoy graphic novels. The only problem was having enough for all students to enjoy. Accessibility can be a problem. Taking a look at what Norton (2003) found offers one possible solution. Basically, Norton found a community of Archie comic book readers in her research. This community shared and even traded comic books. She writes, "The children in the study borrowed comics from one another, went to one another's houses to swap comics, and talked about the stories on a regular basis" (143). Imagine this same scenario within the classroom! For that to happen, comic books must be accessible in the classroom. Invite students to bring in and share any humorous texts they have, creating a text swap in the classroom to make even more texts accessible.

To Help Children Develop an Understanding of Intertextuality

Intertextuality can be found in different ways with humorous texts. Sometimes it's with a familiar character who's a bit silly, or is an odd bird, as Tacky the Penguin has been described. Readers can see similarities among Tacky and other characters that they find funny, such as Lilly from *Chester's Way* (Henkes 1988) and *Lilly's Purple Plastic Purse* (Henkes 1996) and the pigeon in *Don't Let the Pigeon Drive the Bus* (Willems 2003) and *The Pigeon Finds a Hot Dog* (Willems 2004).

Connections can be made with stories and plots as well. Dav Pilkey's *Dog Breath* (1994) and the recent and popular book *Walter the Farting Dog* (Kotzwinkle and Murray 2001) are very similar in their story lines. Both have dogs that have a peculiar problem. Hally Tosis in *Dog Breath* has, you guessed it, bad breath, while Walter, as you may have guessed from the title, has issues with farting too much. When paired together, these two books can help students make connections between what the dogs do, how the families try to keep them, and how they are "saved" in the end.

Readers also make connections with other forms of text, be they movies, television shows, or other written texts. Comparing the voice one uses when reading a written text to a movie character's voice students have heard is one example. For instance, in Matthew's research, Danielle, a third grader, described how she used a voice from a bird in the movie *The Emperor's New Groove* as the voice for the parrot in *Radio Fifth Grade* (Korman 1989), a book she was reading. She was using one text to help her read a new one (Zbaracki 2003).

To Address the Oversimplification of Leveling Systems Often Used to Determine Which Books Children Should Read

Many times, the number of words on a page or where the words are placed on a page are used to determine reading level. How unfortunate for many readers. For instance, *Dog Breath* (Pilkey 1994) has very few words on a page, making the book appear to be an easy read that could potentially be assigned a low level. Upon closer examination of the words, we see that the book should be placed at a much higher level because readers have to go beyond mere word calling to recognize and comprehend the multiple meanings of words and how Pilkey uses them to create humor.

And think about what happens to comics! Many times, they are mistakenly given the same level. Cary (2004), however, helps us see that nothing could be further from the truth. In his words, "Comics range from laid-back easy to big sweat difficult and everything in between. Text-to-picture ratio, the average amount of written text per page or panel in a comic, varies widely. As a general rule, as it varies, so does vocabulary load and the number and complexity of grammar structures" (55). So while comics might be looked upon as having a very easy reading level, they are actually much more challenging. As with *Dog Breath,* readers might be able to call all the words, but they might not be able to comprehend them. These two examples show that leveling humorous texts is anything but simple.

How Might They Be Used?

Read-aloud: Many different authors write humorous texts, and the read-aloud is a perfect time to expose children to some of these authors. Gordon Korman, Sid Fleischman, Jon Scieszka, and Stephen Manes all aim to write humorous texts. Once a reader connects with one of or more of these authors, she is more apt to seek out other books they have written. The read-aloud also affords a teacher with time to discuss texts with children, inviting them to tell what they find funny and why they found the particular event funny.

Shared reading: Shared reading is a time for the children and teacher to read together. Unlike the read-aloud, however, the shared reading experience is designed around a teaching point. In the case of humorous texts, for example, we might want to teach students how to pay attention to both the visual and the written aspect of a comic strip. To do so, we might display different comic strips on an overhead transparency so that all children can see. We can then read the strips to the children. Finally, we might show some other comic strips with the words blacked out. We can have students look at a strip and state what they think should go in each segment of the strip. We can then read the strip to the children, inviting them to chime in when they feel comfortable enough to do so.

Guided reading: How often have you scrounged to find multiple copies of a text to use for a guided reading lesson, only to come up one or two books short? Have you ever thought about using comic books? Imagine the smiles of delight on the students' faces as you show them the comics that they will be reading during their reading lesson with you! There are numerous skills we can teach using comics, such as sequencing, reading vocabulary, and using context clues to identify new words. We agree with Cary, who notes that "comics provide authentic language-learning opportunities for all students" (2004, 15). Cary makes clear that comic books can provide a myriad of opportunities to teach various reading strategies. As with any lesson that carries the guided reading label, however, a particular skill or strategy would become the focus for that one guided reading experience. Say, for example, that you want to teach students how to predict what might happen by skimming through the comic book before reading it. You would model for students how to skim and how to make a prediction based on what you have seen. You would then invite children to do the same. Finally, you would have children read the comic to themselves, providing assistance as needed.

Independent reading: Humorous texts are found in a variety of formats—picture books, novels, comic books (and comic strip anthologies), riddle and joke books, and graphic novels, to name just a few. Therefore, readers have a lot of humorous text options available during independent reading time. During independent reading time, children tend to choose books that make them laugh, as John mentions in the quote at the beginning of the chapter. Thus, the joy of reading will be heard as children chuckle their way through independent reading.

Using Humorous Texts with Younger Elementary-Aged Readers

Jacque is a second-grade teacher who knows that children need to use a variety of reading strategies to best comprehend their texts. Today she is going to explicitly teach some of her students to use visualizing when reading. She picked many different picture book characters who are quite memorable to help her do just that: Tacky the Penguin (Lester 1998, 2005), Lilly from *Lilly's Purple Plastic Purse* (Henkes 1996) and *Lilly's Big Day* (Henkes 2006), and Beans the dog from *A Fine, Fine School* (Creech 2001). Jacque calls the children together and engages them in a conversation about how authors often use words to help readers picture what they are writing about. She further explains that readers need to use the words to create the pictures so that they can better understand the text and so that they can find the text more enjoyable. She then provides them some practice with visualizing through listening. That is, using the selected story characters, she describes each to the students and invites them to draw what the characters look like based on her descriptions. After the drawings are complete, Jacque provides time for the students to share their drawings with one another. Children notice that their drawings are alike yet different. Jacque points out to students that they all have the basic ideas but they look a little different because people draw differently. She also informs the students that sometimes drawings are different because the illustrators have different life experiences.

Carrying this to the reading for the day, Jacque comments, "The same is true with reading. You have your own experiences and that's why when you read the author's words, you might draw a different picture in your mind than someone else. Let's give it a try." She then has children read the part of a story that describes a character and has them draw what they see. She then has students explain why they drew what they drew.

Using Humorous Texts with Older Elementary-Aged Readers

Marv Glotch, who has been teaching for more than thirty years, is quick to capitalize on the use of humorous texts in his classroom. He is well aware of how humorous texts can help develop his fifth-grade students' vocabulary, among other reading skills.

Because puns require readers to know multiple meanings of words, Marv selects picture books such as *Parts* (1997), *More Parts* (2001), and *Even More Parts* (2004), by Tedd Arnold, to introduce his lesson on puns. Marv selects a page from *Even More Parts* that talks about all the figures of speech that involve lips. He reads the page to his class, "Don't give me any of your lip!" "Loose lips sink ships," and "My lips are sealed." He leads the class in a discussion about figurative language. They discuss how each "lip sentence" is an expression and not meant to be taken literally. He explains to the class that the expression "My lips are sealed" does not actually mean the person's lips are sealed, but that the person won't tell certain information to anyone else.

Marv continues the lesson by stating that authors sometimes use figurative language to create humor. He shows students another example from the Amelia Bedelia books, which has Amelia's boss telling her to draw the drapes (Parish 2005). The picture in the book shows Amelia drawing a picture of the curtains. Marv explains how some words have multiple meanings, and when you take the words or expressions literally, they are funny.

He points out to his students that they can look for uses of figurative language so that they can better understand the author's intended message. Marv also stresses that recognizing figurative language is important for critical reading. He reminds his students they need to be savvy readers in order to find the hidden humor.

Sample Titles

Picture Books

Title	Author	Publisher/Year ISBN	Suggested Grade Levels
Good Boy, Fergus!	Shannon, D.	Scholastic/2006 0439490278	K–2
Don't Let the Pigeon Drive the Bus	Willems	Hyperion Books for Children/ 2003 078681988X	K–3
Chicken and Cat	Varon	Scholastic/2006 0439634067	1–3
Lilly's Big Day	Henkes	Greenwillow/2006 0060742364	1–3
Lilly's Purple Plastic Purse	Henkes	Greenwillow/1996 0688128971	1–3
Tacky the Penguin	Lester	Houghton Mifflin/1988 0395455367	1–4

Title	Author	Publisher/Year ISBN	Suggested Grade Levels
Do Not Open This Book!	Muntean	Scholastic/2006 0439698391	2–4
A Fine, Fine School	Creech	Joanna Cotler/HarperCollins/ 2001 006027736X	2–4
Even More Parts	Arnold	Dial Books for Young Readers/2004 0803729383	2–5
More Parts	Arnold	Dial Books for Young Readers/2001 0803714173	2–5
Parts	Arnold	Dial Books for Young Readers/1997 0803720416	2–5
Arnie the Doughnut	Keller	Henry Holt/2003 0805062831	2–6
Comic Adventures of Boots	Kitamura	Farrar, Straus, Giroux/2002 0374314551	3–6
"It Was a Dark and Silly Night"	Spiegelman and Mouly	HarperCollins/2003 0060286288	3–6

Novels

Title	Author	Publisher/ Year ISBN/	Suggested Grade Levels
Amelia Bedelia (series)	Parish	HarperTrophy	2–4
Captain Underpants (series)	Pilkey	Scholastic	2–5
Be a Perfect Person in Just Three Days	Manes	Bantam Doubleday Dell Books for Young Readers/ 1996 0440413494	3–5
The Chicken Doesn't Skate	Korman	Scholastic/1996 05090853007	3–5
Humbug Mountain	Fleischman	Little, Brown/1978 0316285692	3–5
Make Four Million Dollars by Next Thursday	Manes	Bantam Doubleday Dell Books for Young Readers/ 1991 0440413702	3–5

Title	Author	Publisher/ Year ISBN/	Suggested Grade Levels
Sideways Stories from Wayside School	Sachar	HarperTrophy/2003 9780380698714	3–5
Time Warp Trio (series)	Scieszka	Viking & Puffin	3–5
An Almost Perfect Game	Manes	Scholastic/1995 0590444328	4–6
Bandit's Moon	Fleischman	Greenwillow/1998 0688158307	4–6
Chancy and the Grand Rascal	Fleischman	Little, Brown/1966 0688149235	4–6
Mr. Mysterious and Company	Fleischman	Little, Brown/1962 0688149227	4–6
No Coins, Please	Korman	Scholastic/1984 0812436628	4–6
Radio Fifth Grade	Korman	Scholastic/1989 0590419277	4–6
No More Dead Dogs	Korman	Hyperion/2002 0786816015	5–7
Phantom Tollbooth	Juster	Random House/1961 0394820371	5–7
Son of the Mob	Korman	Hyperion/2002 0786807695	7–12

Conclusions

There are many benefits to using humorous texts in the classroom. Probably the number one factor is motivation, both intrinsic and social (Zbaracki 2003). Reading motivation is a key element found in engaged readers (Wigfield 2000; Guthrie and Anderson 1999), and as we illustrate in this chapter, humorous texts are a sure way to enhance motivation. This alone is reason enough for using humorous texts. But another more social reason for using them is that laughter is contagious. Hearing their classmates laugh will help other readers to become interested in reading the same funny text. Soon you will hear a classroom full of laughter—and see a classroom full of engaged readers.

Websites

www.guysread.com is Jon Scieszka's website to help promote reading for boys. There are a lot of humorous titles listed as well as activities and stories for boys.

www.surfnetkids.com/comics.htm is a site for all comic strip lovers. This site provides links to all of your favorite comics. It also has links for teachers for different classroom activities.

www.readwritethink.org/student_mat/student_material_print.asp?id= 21 is a great resource for teachers. It provides an activity for children to create their own comics. The ReadWriteThink site also has many other worthwhile teaching ideas.

www.jokesbykids.com contains jokes submitted by kids, just as the website's name indicates. It's an excellent place for children to share and find jokes. There are also links to other jokes sites.

www.cdli.ca/CITE/cartooning.htm is an incredible site for students! This site tells anything and everything they need to know about creating their own cartoons and comics. It includes links to websites featuring well-known comic strips as well.

CHAPTER 8

Dramatic Texts

Drama engages students with literature in a way that simply reading printed words cannot. —John Kornfeld and Georgia Leyden, "Acting Out: Literature, Drama, and Connecting with History"

What is drama but life with the dull bits cut out. —Alfred Hitchcock

A Brief Description

Dramatic texts provide a unique genre for readers to experience. In this chapter we focus on texts that are written in script format. Script format can appear in two layouts. The first is plays, which are written by an author for performance. The second is readers' theatre, which allows readers the opportunity to create their own scripts, usually based upon an already written text. In a play, the lines and parts are written to be memorized and performed. Readers' theatre puts more stress on reading the lines with expression. While plays don't have to be performed, their meaning is often conveyed by placing the written dialogue in context with scenery, costumes, lighting, sound effects, and props, extending the words. The text actually contains directions on how to create those supporting features. Readers' theatre relies only minimally on external components. It is the reading of the words that carries the burden of conveying meaning. In Figure 8.1 we highlight the differences and similarities between plays and readers' theatre.

Figure 8.1 *Likenesses and Differences Between Plays and Readers' Theatre*

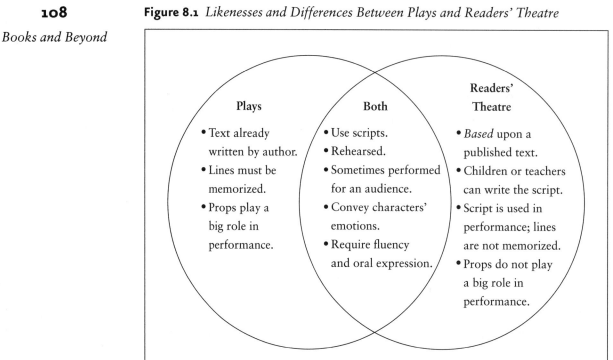

Plays

- Text already written by author.
- Lines must be memorized.
- Props play a big role in performance.

Both

- Use scripts.
- Rehearsed.
- Sometimes performed for an audience.
- Convey characters' emotions.
- Require fluency and oral expression.

Readers' Theatre

- *Based* upon a published text.
- Children or teachers can write the script.
- Script is used in performance; lines are not memorized.
- Props do not play a big role in performance.

Using plays as reading texts and using plays as performance pieces are two ways to engage students with plays, and in this chapter we show that both ways are beneficial. Certainly any play that is performed has to be read, but plays can be read and enjoyed without being performed. In fact, time and resource constraints almost guarantee that it would be impossible to perform every play read in a classroom.

Why Use Them?

There are many reasons for using plays. First, plays are written in a unique script format that is quite different from the formats authors use to write narrative, informational, and poetic texts. The only way students can be exposed to script format is through plays. Students must encounter plays early in their reading programs if they are to build the foundation for understanding often needed later for great works in classical and contemporary literature. Developing an appreciation for and a love of plays, from Greek dramas to the works of Arthur Miller, from Shakespeare to August Wilson, depends significantly on being able to handle the script format. Readers need to be able to understand stories that are told almost entirely through dialogue, which is different than understanding stories that are told in the more traditional narrative style. Likewise, having to fill in a sense of the settings and actions by reading set directions is quite different than having them revealed to you through a narrative text.

Second, exposure to script format is critical if students are going to be engaged in writing original plays or adapting existing works. If students never see plays in print, it probably shouldn't surprise us if it doesn't occur to them to express themselves in this format. Plays offer many writing opportunities for students. For example, plays can be a viable option for students to use during writers' workshop. Plays can also be the format students choose to use when responding to a text. Then, too, students might want to turn a narrative text into a play to share with others. Writing a script might also be a way to innovate on an original text when creating a sequel or a new ending. And think of how powerful plays can be in helping children comprehend nonfiction. Historical events and scientific concepts, for example, might be more memorable if students write them in play format and perform the plays for others.

Third, plays get readers actively involved with the text. This is especially true when the plays are performed. Since individual readers play a role in the scene being read, readers feel as if they are truly a part of the story. Becoming actively involved in the performance naturally encourages readers to think more deeply about the text. Involvement with the text and the characters leads to greater reading enjoyment. Kornfeld and Leyden describe this: "It was great fun for [the students] to immerse themselves in the roles of the characters they were portraying" (2005, 233–34). What better way to make reading fun and to engage children with the text?

Fourth, plays can help children develop reading fluency, one attribute of effective reading (Jenkins 2004; Sloyer 2003; Fredericks 2002). Fluency is built through repeated readings, and plays lend themselves to purposeful repeated readings. Repeated readings allow readers get comfortable with the vocabulary and offer time for students to comprehend the author's intended message. As fluency is enhanced through repeated readings, readers have more mental energy remaining to think more deeply about the play and the characters they are to become when performing the play to an interested audience. Readers can now think critically about the characters' feelings and emotions. By performance time, then, readers will be able to create their interpretations of the characters and convey these interpretations to the audience.

In addition to these reasons are those we mention in Chapter 1. Let's take a look at how these apply to using dramatic texts.

To Better Motivate All Readers

Plays have the potential to motivate all readers. In terms of the specific profiles noted in Chapter 1, the primary group that this genre promises to motivate is the "Reading is not very important to me" profile, as children who match this profile tend to be more interested in social interaction. In fact, Smith and Wilhelm (2002) report that the socially motivated boys in their study described how much they enjoyed the drama activities they did in school. Plays provide the opportunity for this motivating social interaction. Without a doubt, the successful performance of a play relies on collective efforts (Kornfeld and Leyden 2005; Sloyer 2003; Fredericks 2002). The play must be rehearsed with other readers if the characters are going to fit with one another to present a comprehensible performance. If readers are motivated to work with one another, as Worthy and Prater (2002) found, plays are a natural fit.

To Shed Light on the Complexity of Reading

Plays serve as reminders that reading is complex. For example, plays present readers with two unique challenges. First, understanding dialogue—how it is used and why it is used—is critical in order to best comprehend the play. It is primarily through dialogue that readers learn about the characters and how they interact with one another. It's through the dialogue that insights into the plot are revealed. Some plays will prominently feature a narrator who may explicitly make these elements obvious to the reader, but many will not. Students need to be taught about how the narrator provides the reader with information that is critical for understanding and how to uncover this information in the dialogue of the characters when a narrator is not present in a play. Second, understanding stage directions is another challenge unique to plays. Sometimes the stage directions directly state story elements (e.g., Ohio, 1800s). Most often, children need to be taught how to read stage directions and how they relate to the overall play. Without narrative description to extend what is being said by the characters, readers might overlook some critical aspects of the story.

Another way that plays show the complexity of reading is through the way that story elements are portrayed. In order to understand the entire play or scene being presented, readers must understand specific story elements such as settings and characters (Sloyer 2003). The latter involves understanding not only the traits of the character in focus but the traits of those with whom the character is interacting. Readers must understand the characters' motivations, goals, and conflicts. Readers also have to constantly monitor their comprehension as they read the play with others. They must be thinking about what is happening in the story and why.

And, if we think about how reading is related to the other language arts, plays may be one of the best texts to bring together all the language arts (i.e., reading, writing, speaking, listening, and viewing). Throughout any given performance, for example, readers must not just read the script but actively listen to other performers and speak their parts (Kornfeld and Leyden 2005).

To Expand Children's Understandings of the Variety of Text Genres and Structures

Plays are basically scripts. Many readers are unfamiliar with this text format because they lack exposure to it. Rarely do we see students self-select scripts for independent reading. Incorporating plays into the reading program, then, may provide students their first exposure to the format and heighten their awareness of unique features such as the role of a narrator and what the notes on the script refer to when describing stage movement. Understanding this format can make reading it less uncomfortable for readers. Take a look at the first few lines in the play by Sharon Creech in her novel *Replay* (2005b).

> *At the exterior of a tumbledown cabin with a porch. Trees surrounding, one of which is hollow. As the curtain opens, old* Rumpopo *is standing on the porch, facing audience, talking to himself.*
>
> Rumpopo: Aye, my bones ache. My life is empty. It is over. What use is there for an old man like me?
>
> (*Enter the children.* Lucia, *and* Pahchay, *and their dog. They look worn and bedraggled.*)

These few lines alone show how complex scripts can be. Why is part of this in italics? What does that mean? How come the names aren't in italics? Where are the children entering from? All of these questions and more can be confusing to a reader who hasn't seen the script format before. Imagine trying to make sense of the story while also mentally juggling all these other aspects of the format. Some readers might actually find these extra elements distracting; however, using scripts and teaching students how to read them can help them gain confidence in and understanding of the new structure.

After students become comfortable with the structure of scripts they can begin to create their own. Writing the script for a play is a rather daunting task. Beginning with creating scripts for readers' theatre to learn the challenges and joys of writing within this genre seems like a good first step. Readers' theatre provides students with the opportunity to work with a number of different types of texts (picture books, poetry, famous speeches, and song lyrics) when creating a script (Worthy and Prater 2002). Readers can study favorite texts and pull scenes of their choice. While they have the story as a basis for the performance, they can still create their own interpretation of the story. They can include or edit elements from the story. Indeed, experience with creating scripts for readers' theatre may be the best launching point for helping students in their attempts to write a script from scratch. As playwrights, they will have to make decisions like what role a narrator will play in the telling of their story or how explicit to make certain stage directions. Creating a play from the ground up is sure to heighten their awareness of how others do the same when they are reading plays.

To Make More Texts Acceptable and Accessible in and out of School

One problem with plays is they are not very available inside or outside of the classroom. Our observations reveal that readers rarely choose plays as a self-directed form of reading. Certainly accessibility plays a role in that outcome. Plays are not often on the bestseller lists or featured items in book clubs. While the classic works are made available in bookstores, most popular contemporary plays are relegated to a back shelf if included in the inventory at all. The scripts behind popular films and television programs are often novelized—that is, available in narrative stories but not in the original scripted format. If readers do overcome the hurdles and obstacles and actually track down a play they want to read, accepting the text by permitting students to read it seems like a given.

Fortunately, there are several authors of young adult books who are making plays and the understanding of the script format used to write them accessible. Sharon Creech is but one. She uses this format in her most recent book, *Replay* (2005b). *Replay* is about a young boy who struggles to find his place in his family and the world. He finds that he loves the theatre and enjoys being in a school play that his teacher has written. At the end of the book Creech includes the script to the play, which she herself wrote. This book is a perfect example to show readers how the script format fits in the narrative literature they are reading. In Paul Fleischman's book *Seek* (2003), a classroom assignment turns into a radio play, which forms the heart of the book but is just one part of a sound collage that Fleischman weaves together. Other dialogic elements from radio programs form the background noise for this novel presented in a script format. In both *Monster* (1991) and *Shooter* (2004b), Walter Dean Myers tells his stories of contemporary events by using various formats including court transcripts, interview transcriptions, and movie screenplays. Lauren Myracle tells her stories in *ttyl* (2005) and *ttfn* (2006) entirely in text messages, which form the script for these novels. Books like these may increase the frequency with which plays find their way into the reading habits of students because they expose children to this often forgotten genre.

Perhaps one of the easiest ways to make plays and scripts both acceptable and accessible is to embrace the current attraction of readers' theatre. With increased attention to fluency and the instructional role that readers' theatre plays in addressing this element in reading, an abundance of commercial materials are now available for classroom teachers. These materials can certainly be used selectively to engage readers in independent work away from the teacher as they prepare readers' theatre performances. Even better than the commercial materials, though, are the scripts that students themselves create. Almost *anything* can be turned into a script. Sloyer writes, "A story, a poem, a scene from a play, a letter, even a song lyric provide the ingredients for the script" (2003, 3). We can encourage students to bring in a variety of texts to use as catalysts for creating their own scripts, conveying the acceptance and value of these texts simultaneously. Because student-created scripts are based on texts that interest and validate students, they give the students a better sense of ownership. The script is *their* creation. That is where the ownership begins. When the students have the chance to perform their script in front of an audience, they want the presentation be a success.

Yet another way to make scripts accessible is to collect the student-created scripts and put them in three-ring binders. Once assembled, the scripts can go on the classroom bookshelves along with the other texts in the classroom, making them available for students to read. An additional spin-off of having student-created scripts available for all to read is that readers are able to see what their peers are doing and what their scripts look like, providing ideas for future scriptwriting. These ideas can lead to an ongoing production of new scripts by an increasing number of students. Can you imagine the purposeful reading, writing, speaking, and listening that would result from their creations?

To Help Children Develop an Understanding of Intertextuality

Opportunities to foster intertextuality abound in the use of plays in a classroom reading program. One of the best ways is to choose scenes in different plays that follow a specific theme. Whether the theme is friendship, adventure, mystery, or humor, having students choose scenes that relate to a theme is an easy way to help establish connections among texts.

Plays can also be connected in many different ways beyond their themes. For example, students can read plays written by the same playwright and identify connections across plays. Or perhaps plays written during a similar time period can be connected by examining how they reflect the issues and events of that time. Then, too, certain plays actually pay homage to the same classical play on which they are based. Think of the list of plays and stories that owe their foundational ideas to *Romeo and Juliet*. There are references in plays to other literary works and there are references to plays in other literary works.

Readers' theatre and student-written scripts are additional ways to foster intertextuality among texts in a classroom. Kornfeld and Leyden (2005) provide examples of how this happened in their use of readers' theatre scripts in the classroom. Their readers created scripts based on a slavery theme. Students found nonfiction texts, picture books, and novels that covered the chosen topic. When students created their scripts they cross-referenced information from a number of different sources. Clearly, Kornfeld and Leyden offer an excellent example of how readers can be led to make connections among multiple texts during the process of creating scripts for a readers' theatre performance.

To Address the Oversimplification of Leveling Systems Often Used to Determine Which Books Children Should Read

Plays present advantages when it comes to matching texts to students. For instance, plays are written with multiple parts. Those parts often vary in size. As Worthy and Prater (2002) observe, while the reading level of the total script might be beyond the reach of some students, a part within the play might not be. Teachers can strategically assign parts so that all students can make a successful contribution to the reading of the play. In other words, all students can be reading the same text, but the teacher can differentiate by assigning students different parts. Doing so provides students with a meaningful purpose for the reading and rereading of the play. Students who most value the experience will be better engaged and perform above expected levels (Worthy and Prater 2002).

Student-created scripts such as the one on slavery described by Kornfeld and Leyden are often based on so many different texts that leveling won't be as obvious as with other genres. To address the wide range of reading levels that exist within any given classroom of readers, we can show students how to adapt everything from picture books to novel excerpts into scripts. In both cases, whether the plays are published or student scripted, the texts cannot be simplified to *one* reading level. Instead, a range of reading levels is represented. In fact, they may be the best vehicles to use to group students together by factors other than levels. Yes, using plays can tear down the walls created by reading levels and open up this dramatic genre to all readers.

How Might They Be Used?

Read-aloud: A play may be a challenging text to use as a read-aloud. The words are written to be heard aloud, but the challenge is being able to orally distinguish one character from another for an audience primarily relying on audio clues. Teachers with sophisticated oral-interpretation skills may have no trouble doing this, but it could be a significant challenge for many.

Plays are a genre that allows the students to actually be *a part* of the read-aloud. Most often the read-aloud is a time when the teacher reads to students. However, a play provides you with the chance to find a script that has a part for *every* child in the class. You can first read the script aloud as the class follows along. Doing so would help familiarize students with the story. Next, you assign roles and individual students can practice reading their designated parts. Finally, the class can come together, and each person, in turn, can read the script aloud. In the end the class is actively involved in reading the script. More formal performances of plays are another alternative to traditional read-aloud experiences. Save some of your read-aloud time for students to present scenes they have rehearsed from plays they are reading. You can also use these same techniques for sharing student-written scripts in readers' theatre presentations.

Shared reading: Shared reading provides an opportunity for you to begin to teach about the major components that distinguish script formats. One way to introduce the idea of parts or roles in a script is with a book such as *What! Cried Granny: An Almost Bedtime Story* (Lum 1998). Begin by reading the book aloud to the entire class. Your initial discussion might focus on how the book can be divided into three parts (roles): the granny, the boy, and a narrator. As you read the book aloud to the class a second time, the students become more familiar with how the story can be read in script parts. That is, during the second reading, move from modeling to guiding, using prompts and probes to see if the students understand how to use the unique features of script structure to understand who is speaking. Once students seem ready, divide the class into groups of three and assign parts so students can read the text more independently, trying to apply what they have learned without as much teacher support. Both in the large group and as students work independently, ask questions related to how characters are feeling, why they might be feeling that way, how they might talk with one another, and how to listen to each character to know when it is their character's turn to speak. Using a book such as this is a good way to introduce the concept of script parts using a format students already know (picture books). Using a script for a shared reading lesson also provides readers with a natural opportunity to read aloud and interact with others.

Guided reading: Do plays work well as material for guided reading? You bet they do! If you can find an appropriate play at the instructional level of the readers, there is nothing inherent in these texts that would preclude them from guided reading. All the typical instructional techniques used during guided reading can be used with plays. All the learner outcomes sought from guided reading can occur with plays. In fact, plays can offer teachers a few additional benefits if used during guided reading. For example, because plays do not represent a single reading level but actually are composed of parts at different reading levels, you can put together guided reading groups that are based less on strict levels and more about similar needs or interests. As with the multilevel texts discussed earlier in this book (see Chapter 4), the use of plays can be a good way to actually shake up the membership of guided reading groups that may be growing a bit stagnant. The other advantage of plays is that they are structured for oral performance in a way that avoids round-robin reading. Instead of each student waiting to read one chunk of the text sequentially or listening to each student read the whole text, students must pay close attention to know when it is their turn to read their part. This is purposeful oral reading at its best. After strategically assigning parts, invite students to practice their parts, providing support more directly to those students who need it. While listening to students rehearse their parts, you can also assess their oral reading, taking a running record on that assigned part of the play. After students practice with and away from the teacher, the group can perform the oral reading of the whole text, with each reader contributing his or her part.

Independent reading: If plays and scripts are added to the mix of reading materials available in a classroom library, there should be no reason they can't find their way into students' hands for independent reading. At this point, we may need to be a bit proactive about searching for and securing texts written in script formats. As more and more authors of children's books experiment with this format, searching out these books will be less difficult. In the meantime, commercially available scripts designed for readers' theatre presentations might be used to fill this void (see the sample titles and websites at the end of this chapter for some suggestions). The idea of collecting and providing access to student-written scripts might also be a way of making sure plays are available for independent reading.

Plays can be a good vehicle for heterogeneously grouping students for independent work. First, the multilevel nature of the scripts means that students reading at different levels can work together on preparing for a performance if parts are strategically assigned. Second, preparing a play for performance includes other aspects requiring skills that go beyond expertise in handling print. Students with other talents could find outlets for their skills in helping get the other aspects of the play ready to support the performance of the script.

Using Dramatic Texts with Younger Elementary-Aged Readers

In looking ahead in her anthology, Janet discovers that an upcoming lesson suggests a response project that includes turning the anthology selection into a puppet play. She likes the idea and sees the motivational and instructional value of having her second-grade students prepare for a performance. The preparation will provide meaningful practice for fluency, encourage positive social interaction, and engage her students in productive independent work while she works with small groups and individuals. However, she anticipates that her students have had little experience in working with characters and using oral expression to convey a sense of those characters to an audience. She decides to do a shared reading lesson on this strategy.

Janet realizes that a book she has previously read aloud is a good resource for modeling and practicing this strategy. She grabs the book *What's the Time, Grandma Wolf?* by Ken Brown (2001), a favorite of her students. She brings her students to the carpet and reintroduces the book to them. She tells them to listen carefully for how the author gives a word clue about how the seven different characters each ask Grandma Wolf, "What's the time?" Brown effectively structured his book so that brave Piglet shouted, shy Fawn whispered, noisy Crow squawked, sassy Squirrel squeaked, Badger barked, Duckling quacked, and Rabbit giggled. Janet begins the rereading, carefully placing a strong emphasis on each of the descriptive words and then modeling how her voice changes. On a second rereading, she invites the children to chime in on the phrase "What's the time, Grandma Wolf?" with reminders to listen to the word clues on how each character would say the phrase. Before a third reading, she hands out index cards, each with the name of a character written on it, to seven children. She rereads the book a third time and invites those students assigned character parts to add the repeated phrase to the story. She reminds them again to listen to the word clues before they say the line as their character would. Knowing that her other students will also want turns, she promises that they will try this again during shared reading. She also tells them that in case students want to try this on their own, she will leave the book and the cards in the theatre corner, where students can practice this activity during independent time.

Using Dramatic Texts with Older Elementary-Aged Readers

Sara is a fourth-grade teacher who loves new and creative ideas. She has been to the International Reading Association's (IRA) annual conference a couple of times. One presentation she was able to attend was with authors Avi and Katherine Paterson, who were doing readers' theatre presentations using their own work. She enjoyed how the authors took a common text and performed it together. She paid close attention to how the readers worked with one another and were able to capture the feeling of the characters they were reading. Upon arriving back at school after the conference, she was eager to implement this idea in her classroom.

Excited about the idea, she describes the presentation to her class. She asks her students if they would like to try the idea as well. They clamor with excitement and she proceeds with the activity. Sara pulls some books that she has already read aloud to the class so they are already familiar with the text. She pulls titles by Avi, Katherine Paterson, Gordon Korman, and Kevin Henkes. She tells her students to get into groups of four or five. She asks them to find their favorite scenes from one of the books based on the theme of friendship.

After each group finds a scene it likes, Sara introduces how to write a script for readers' theatre. She stresses how important it is that the dialogue describe what is going on in the scene. Using the example "It was a dark and stormy night," Sara writes how one character might say, "Wow, the thunder sure is loud tonight," and another character could reply with, "Yes, and I think it's been raining for a good hour. I don't think it's going to let up anytime soon."

Sara points out how the students can use actual dialogue from the book, or they can create their own dialogue for the script. She stresses the importance of using dialogue to describe the details of what is going on in the scene. She then provides the rest of the class time for the students to begin writing their scripts. Understanding that this activity takes time, Sara gives two days for the groups to write their scripts. Each group then spends a couple of days rehearsing its script.

At the end of the week, Sara decides it's time for her class to perform for an audience. At first each group presents to the entire class. Then Sara invites the class' kindergarten reading buddies to attend a second round of performances. Sara is so excited by the success of the performances that she decides to take the show on the road. Now her class has performances scheduled at nursing homes and community centers (Jenkins 2004).

Sample Titles: Books That Involve Scripts

Title	Author	Publisher/Year ISBN	Suggested Grade Levels
What's the Time, Grandma Wolf?	Brown	Peachtree/2001 1561452505	1–3
Frog Went A-Courting	Catalano	Boyds Mills/1998 1563976374	2–3
Show Time at the Polk Street School: Plays You Can Do Yourself or in the Classroom	Giff	Delacorte/1992 0385307942	2–4
What! Cried Granny: An Almost Bedtime Story	Lum	Dial/1998 0803723822	2–4
You're On! Seven Plays in English and Spanish	Carlson	Morrow Junior/1999 0688162371	4–6
Novio Boy	Soto	Harcourt/1997 0152015310	5–7
Replay	Creech	Joanna Cotler/2005 0060540192	5–7
Seek	Fleischman	Simon Pulse/2003 0689854021	6–8

Title	Author	Publisher/Year ISBN	Suggested Grade Levels
Monster	Myers	Amistad/2001 0064407314	6–9
ttfn	Myracle	Amulet/2006 0810959712	8–10
ttyl	Myracle	Harry N. Abrams/2005 0810987880	8–10
Shooter	Myers	Amistad/2004 0064472906	9 and up

Conclusions

Throughout this chapter we describe the many uses and benefits of including dramatic texts in the classroom. Readers are motivated by this dramatic format because its potential for performance offers a more purposeful reason for reading. Plays provide an inherent opportunity for the social interaction that is attractive to so many readers. While it may be a new format for some readers, it is a format they are likely to encounter at some point in their school careers. It is important that they are exposed to scripts early in their reading programs in order to learn more about the unique text structure and how to use features of the structure to gain a deeper understanding and appreciation for these works. Making students aware of these features better ensures that they will be more knowledgeable on how to write scripts and plays, adding an option for their own writing and growth as writers. Working with this genre encourages readers to be more fluent readers and invites them to critically analyze texts and to make connections to other texts. Perhaps including dramatic plays in your classroom will inspire the next great playwright!

Websites

www.aaronshep.com/rt is a website by author Aaron Shepard designed to help teachers learn about and utilize readers' theatre in the classroom.

www.geocities.com/pocolocoplayers/child.html, which is also known as Freedrama.com, is a good site for classroom ideas for using plays. It has an extensive list of free play scripts that teachers can use.

www.childdrama.com/mainframe.html has several useful teacher links. It has lesson plans and teacher tips for using plays in the classroom. There is also a list of play scripts that are available for purchase.

www.poetryalive.com is a website about poetry, but we had to include it here because it provides two books of scripted poems for both older and younger readers. You'll also find a wealth of other resources sure to boost your enthusiasm for including plays (and poetry) in your reading program.

www.readwritethink.org/lessons/lesson_view.asp?id=310 contains a good lesson plan for helping students delve more deeply into characters from a book. The lesson is designed to teach them how to interpret characters and to express that creatively through drama.

www.teachingheart.net/readerstheater.htm has a long list of scripts that are ready to print out. It also provides activities and tips for using readers' theatre. There is also an assessment form that can be adapted for classroom use.

9

Real-Life Texts

If teachers can tap into existing student interests, tap the conditions of flow to develop and sustain new ones and show students the connection of learning to their lives, the data here suggest that even resistant students can become engaged learners.

—Michael Smith and Jeffrey Wilhelm, *"Reading Don't Fix No Chevys"*

[B]y letting the literacy practices in which our students revel outside of the classroom count for something in the classroom—perhaps we can help students see what they do in school counts as real life.

—Sean Cavazos-Kottke, "Tuned Out But Turned On"

A Brief Description

While any text might be considered a real-life text, including all those previously described in this book, in this chapter we want to examine written materials that primarily serve a function in nonschool settings. These materials are not intentionally designed for classroom instructional purposes. In this chapter, we classify real-life texts into the following categories:

▪ environmental print (e.g., billboards and advertisements)

▪ materials that assist us to cope with the complexities of life (e.g., directions, manuals, menus)

- materials that help us deal with time and space (e.g., bus schedules, maps)

- materials that help us build a sense of community within and across groups (e.g., print at celebrations, sporting events, political rallies)

As you can see from the examples, many of these texts are not in a book format, yet they provide sources of reading nonetheless. The examples also help illustrate that real-life texts are readily available, often at no or little cost.

Why Use Them?

Lori Norton-Meier (2004, 260) tells a story about driving with her daughter and being asked, "Mom, what does that bumper sticker mean . . . 'The media are only as liberal as the conservative businesses that own them.'"

"What do you think it means?" Lori asked.

"Well, it is kind of confusing. You always hear people complain about the liberal press. But that bumper sticker uses the word *only,* which is mixing me up." Then she paused and said: "Well, I think it means that how can something be liberal when the people who own it are just the opposite. I guess it is saying how can the press be liberal when the people who have the money and make the decisions are conservative."

After a few quiet moments, her daughter asked, "Mom, how do you know if what someone puts on a bumper sticker is true? Are the media really owned by conservative businesses?"

Lori thought this was a pretty heavy conversation for a short commute home and replied, "I don't know the answer to that; do you think there is a way we could find out?"

At home, they went to the Internet and began a search that led to new questions. The search ended only when it began to interfere with the demands of traditional homework.

Helping a child try to make sense of the political messages of a bumper sticker or watching another comb through direction manuals and cheat-code books to discover how to best the latest game he is trying to learn points to the power of real-life texts as reading motivators. These same students who in other contexts might be less enthused about reading tasks suddenly become engaged, independent, strategic readers as they use real-life texts and strategies to independently solve the problems they encounter in their lives.

Capitalizing on the power of these learning opportunities, then, is the most important reason for moving more real-life texts into the classroom reading program. In addition, we offer the following six reasons for adding the use of real-life texts to a classroom reading program.

To Better Motivate All Readers

Real-life texts are helpful for reaching some of the student profiles defined in Figure 1.1. These texts can be used to target the two hardest groups of students to motivate: the "I hate reading!" and "I don't like reading" groups. A close review of the motivation research reveals that these groups of students scored low on every affective dimension of reading, with the exception of work avoidance. The only distinguishing factor between these groups of students is the degree to which they avoid reading; the former group is more severe than the latter. Students in these groups avoid reading because they no longer have much success with reading. They do not see themselves as inside players anymore, so like most of us, they tend to stay away from something they know they will not have success with. In fact, the more the activity looks like the typical school reading activity, the greater their effort to avoid it will be.

The obvious challenge is how to get any text into these students' hands. If they are not handling text, how do we begin to help them get better at dealing with it? Previously we suggested setting up a display of many different types of texts to entice all students to wander over and put their hands on something, setting a series of events in motion. That is, if we can get them to touch something, we might be able to get them to open it. If we get them to open it, we might be able to get them to try to read it. If we get them to try to read it, we can give them a reason for letting us help them get better at it. So what are these students most likely to touch? We believe those texts that look the least like school reading are the winners.

Real-life texts are good for students on the other end of the motivational continuum—the "My teacher says reading is important" and "I love reading" profiles. When students are primarily reading to be compliant, like the former group, it is important to help them develop a more internal locus of control for their reading activities if we are trying to engender a lifelong reading habit. Showing them materials that aren't assigned by the teacher but still might be interesting and valuable to read begins to help them expand their reading repertoire. For the students who love reading, real-life texts can expand a reading repertoire that may be narrowly focused, bringing a better balance to the texts they are selecting.

Acknowledging the potential useful role of real-life texts in reading programs also acknowledges a more complex view of reading. We've looked at motivation, but what about other reader factors? Smith and Wilhelm (2002) tell the story of a "struggling reader" who doesn't seem to struggle at all when the text he is reading is a repair manual for a car he is working on. Clearly certain real-life texts will allow certain readers to make better use of their subject knowledge, background experience, and technical vocabulary, leading to greater success with reading than traditional school reading activities. Obviously, there is clarity of purpose in the student's head when he is consulting the repair manual that might not be present when he's responding to an assigned selection in an anthology.

Real-life texts also address a variety of text factors. Notice what happens if you bring in a variety of travel guides, brochures, and advertisements focused on a specific country. Each has a connected focus but will vary in the amount and kind of content it covers. Some texts such as travel guides have a greater degree of sophistication in their presentation of information and are more concept dense. Others (e.g., brochures) present less content more directly. Information will also be organized in a variety of formats, some more accessible than others. The purposes might vary from assisting readers with planning a trip to hooking readers into purchasing a package deal. The possibility of a student finding materials that are organized with a set of features that will facilitate greater success with this reading task suddenly becomes higher.

Finally, context factors around the use of real-life texts set up risk-free reading situations for students. Since most readers have selected the text needed to accomplish a specific task, the reading materials are more contextualized and are usually read in a psychologically safe environment. In other words, while real-life reading can take place in contexts that are more stressful than others, the outcome probably won't result in a grade or a test score. Certain outcomes have greater degrees of importance (e.g., discovering how to program an iPod), but that importance is often defined by the reader, not by an external force.

To Expand Children's Understandings of the Variety of Text Genres and Structures

Real-life texts tend to favor informational text structures often not seen in other texts used in instructional settings. We, like Duke (2000), have argued about the importance of integrating more informational texts and therefore offering a more balanced diet of reading experiences to better prepare students to work with nonfiction texts. Integrating real-life texts is one way. While some real-life texts have narrative story lines, like letters or diary entries, or narrative stories embedded in some advertisements or pamphlets, most do not. Like the bumper sticker Lori's daughter was trying to make sense of, many real-life texts convey their messages in single words or short phrases. Take, for example, the Nike slogan "Just Do It!" or Burger King's "Have It Your Way!" Others, such as instruction manuals for assembling a car model or playing a video game, are organized without concern about story development. They offer a wide variety of other structures with which readers need to become familiar.

Real-life texts are good examples of many of the nonfiction structures we discuss in Figure 1.5. That is, *recounts* are seen in letters and journal entries, as writers try to communicate over space and time by retelling events that have happened to them or others. *Procedural* texts are seen in many real-life materials, from recipes to directions on how to assemble a product. And let's remember that real-life examples of procedural texts may be the best way to help students see the need to read carefully and write clearly.

Similarly *sequentially ordered* texts are represented in many real-life texts that have time lines embedded in them, from schedules for television shows to upcoming events at the local theater. When chronology is a critical issue, these texts can help the teacher convey that to the students.

Finally, *persuasive* texts are embedded in most advertisements, as a close look at texts that advocate for specific political issues from interest groups to campaign materials will illustrate. As with procedural texts, persuasive real-life texts can be used as samples or models to help students learn how to read critically and how to craft similar texts to convince others.

To Make More Texts Acceptable and Accessible in and out of School

The use of real-life texts in school reading programs helps us rethink what reading is and what readers are. When we include real-life texts in our definition of reading materials, we also expand our definition of what it means to be a reader. We convey our new definition to students by not only accepting real-life texts but encouraging students to bring them to school. Hence, we make the texts acceptable *and* accessible. Students who avoid the novels sitting inside their desks while they intensively comb through catalogs are readers just as much as the students who choose to read the assigned novels. This expanded definition also calls on us to take a second look at students' perceived reading deficits. That is, a student's deficits in reading can't solely be defined by inability to perform school tasks when a look at the student's literacy life outside of school, reading real-life texts, suggests evidence to the contrary.

To Help Children Develop an Understanding of Intertexuality

When we discuss the importance of making connections between texts, many of us probably don't think about the use of real-life texts in fostering those connections. While other texts may be better for enhancing students' ability to use text-to-text connections to understand, respond to, and compose texts, we need to remember that literary references abound in real-life texts. We can remember the teacher who brought relevancy to a traditional study of mythology by asking us to find embedded references in contemporary advertising. Another teacher sent us on a search to find Shakespeare alive and well in texts that surrounded us. Even the slogans plastered on buttons, T-shirts, bumper stickers, and posters can have their origins in more literary texts. Likewise, popular culture captured in real-life texts can also find its way into those literary texts. Both of these are fitting examples of how students learn to use intertextuality to better understand a given topic.

To Address the Oversimplification of Leveling Systems Often Used to Determine Which Books Children Should Read

Levels rarely come into play when we talk of real-life texts, and readers are all the better for it. Real-life texts remind us that even the simplest of texts can be complicated. While the words on slogans are fairly easy to read (i.e., easy level), for example, fully comprehending and critically reading them is another skill altogether (higher level). So while readers may be able to read a slogan such as "Just Do It!" understanding just what Nike wants them to do is much more complicated. And how refreshing for readers to focus on their purpose for reading rather than on whether their text is at level L or Q! Without a doubt, real-life texts create a wide range of reading levels. On one end, some real-life reading material conveys its message in a single word. On the other end, real-life materials also include sophisticated, complex technical manuals. Real-life materials remind us that the levels we use to classify materials in instructional programs rarely mirror what happens with texts outside of the classroom.

How Might They Be Used?

Read-aloud: Real-life reading materials are fairly limited in their use during read-aloud time. Certainly other materials—trade books, anthology selections, poems—are appropriate texts for introducing students to authors and their texts. Occasionally, however, a narrative story or a poem might be embedded in a real-life text. These can be shared in a read-aloud setting. Certain books are even written in real-life text formats, like diary entries (*Diary of a Worm* [2003] and *Diary of a Spider* [2005], by Cronin) and letters (*Dear Mr. Blueberry* [James 1991]). We can feature these during the read-aloud time.

Shared reading: Real-life reading materials are probably best featured as a part of instruction in shared reading or large-group settings. Real-life materials can be easily integrated into demonstrations of strategies. In fact, real-life materials might be the best materials to show why, when, and how strategies should be used. Students who often see a strong disconnect between reading in school and reading in the world beyond school will be better able to make connections between them if they see applications of reading instruction used with real-life reading materials.

Real-life texts may be best used in whole-class instruction as models for helping students become familiar with nonfiction structures. If the teacher is helping students recognize these structures in the texts they are reading, real-life texts are effective instructional tools. For example, what if students have difficulty following step-by-step directions? Instructions involving real-life procedural texts show more than tell students the need to read carefully and write clearly in their everyday lives. Similarly, real-life texts such as television guides and entertainment sections in the newspaper have time lines embedded in them, from schedules for television shows to upcoming events at the local theater, and lend themselves well to teaching students about sequentially ordered texts. Do you want to strengthen your students' persuasive writing? Looking closely at real-life texts such as pamphlets from advocacy groups that argue for specific points of view can help all students improve their critical analysis and write convincing arguments.

Guided reading: In order to use real-life texts for guided reading, you need to have access to a set of materials so that each student in the small group will have a text in his or her hands. If you cannot obtain enough copies of the same materials, then try to obtain materials that are very similar to each other. They should be at about the same reading level. They also need to lend themselves to instruction focused on the same strategy for understanding or response. For example, if you are focusing on scanning text for information, you might secure multiple copies of the yellow pages so that each student can try out scanning strategies with this real-life text. If you introduced a real-life text as a sample or model during shared reading in the large-group setting, you may have recognized a need to review that lesson with some students in a smaller group. A guided reading group can be the best opportunity to review the use of real-life texts to make sure all students grasped the concepts being presented.

Independent reading: Real-life texts can contribute to the overall independent recreational reading program. Their presence in a classroom leads to a lot of additional independent reading. Here's why: First, they greatly enhance the print-rich nature of classroom environments. That is, strategically selected and placed, real-life texts from the slogans on a teacher's T-shirt to the poster on the classroom door are likely to be repeatedly read by students.

Second, real-life materials can be added to existing literacy centers, becoming what some call literacy props. For example, adding catalogs and ads to a math corner or applications and forms to a writing center often leads to additional reading and writing opportunities. Even with very young children, educators suggest adding real-life texts to play centers. Stroud (1995) suggested adding a variety of real-life texts to the block area to help children see the useful function of print and to encourage self-initiated literacy activities in that center.

Third, entire portable learning stations can be developed around real-life reading materials. Collections of related real-life materials can be placed in tubs that students can take back to their desks or a quiet corner to independently engage in explorations that would provide additional practice with reading and writing skills. Can you imagine students sorting and classifying coupons in one tub or plotting out vacations by looking at travel materials in another?

Finally, some real-life texts are suitable for independent reading. Imagine again those students who might not otherwise stay engaged now using their independent reading time to pore over an owner's manual or a how-to guide.

Using Real-Life Texts with Younger Elementary-Aged Readers

As a first-grade teacher, Stacy is committed to helping her students learn how to become independent learners and strategic problem solvers. She is constantly searching for ideas for keeping young children independently

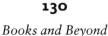

engaged while practicing their literacy skills. She has discovered the idea of creating career boxes. She purchases a few plastic tubs and begins to fill each one with real-life materials with a focus on a specific career. For those interested in the restaurant business, she fills a tub with menus, placemats, napkins, and food containers with logos on them, pads for recording orders, telephone directories with restaurant listings, and other similar materials. By adding some play money and coins and a telephone, she is able to encourage hands-on experiences with math skills as well as reading and writing skills. In another tub, she places materials related to the medical profession such as medical charts, doctor's office forms, patient file folders, brochures and pamphlets, first-aid manuals, and pads of paper for writing out advice. By adding a thermometer, she once again blurs the line between symbol systems. The materials in the career boxes grow as students bring in more items, and the number of career boxes grows as more professions are added. When one box gets a little tired, Stacy retires it for a while and adds a new one to the rotation.

Lori Norton-Meier (2004) used a similar format to work with her students. She wrote a letter to a bumper sticker company and received a box of nearly five hundred bumper stickers. She turned this into a literacy box in her room. She also had literacy boxes filled with pins, menus, tray liners, door hangers, and brochures. Students could select a literacy box, dump out the contents, and engage in conversations about its contents. She encouraged students to compare and contrast items; look for patterns; sort and organize while talking about letters, shapes, colors, and designs; and most importantly, think about their meanings. Discussions of the contents became instructional opportunities for visual literacy (Which bumper sticker stands out to you and why?), critical literacy (What is the message this bumper sticker is promoting?), and personal identity (Which bumper sticker would you put on your car and why?).

Using Real-Life Texts with Older Elementary-Aged Readers

As Michael Ford shared in the introduction, he is amazed by the amount of information and the way it is presented in the forty-four-page, two-by-three-inch instruction booklet that his son Vo voraciously read to solve the vocabulary problem he had with his new Game Boy game *Yu-Gi-Oh! Dark Duel Stories*. Shelley Xu (Xu, Perkins, and Zurich 2005) describes how she capitalizes on the interest in the Yu-Gi-Oh! card game to invite her students to do a compare-contrast activity about the world of Yu-Gi-Oh! and ancient Egypt. Michael agrees that the cards themselves present ample opportunities to springboard into additional reading and writing activities, but he started thinking more about the manuals themselves. Watching Vo use his manual, Michael saw that he began with page 1 and the table of contents. He quickly discovered that the rules for building his deck started on page 13. He jumped to page 44 to find the terms section to see how *deck capacity* was defined. He wandered his way back to page 16, where he learned how to solve his problem about exceeding capacity by reading the explanation in the fine print.

What if a teacher invited a group of students to bring in the manual from a recent game they had purchased? Imagine walking the students through the features of the manuals. By calling attention to these features in their game manuals, the teacher could create an awareness of similar features in school materials. Main topics and supporting ideas with narrative and bulleted items are presented in each section, modeling how to present ideas clearly. You also find diagrams with clearly labeled parts, graphics of cyclical events, and semantic feature analysis charts. In the Yu-Gi-Oh! manual, a section on battle outcomes actually presents an "If . . . then" chart showing cause and effect in mathematical formulas. With a little creativity using the materials students already have and are familiar with, a teacher could design powerful instruction about how to use text features to understand and present important ideas.

Sample Titles

Letters and Postcards

Title	Author	Publisher/Year ISBN	Suggested Grade Levels
Dear Mr. Blueberry	James	Aladdin/1991 0689807686	pre-K–1
The Jolly Postman	Ahlberg and Ahlberg	Little, Brown/1986 0316126446	pre-K–2
Yours Truly, Goldilocks	Flor Ada	Aladdin/1998 0689844522	pre-K–2
Dear Peter Rabbit	Flor Ada	Aladdin/1997 0689812892	pre-K–3
With Love, Little Red Hen	Flor Ada	Aladdin/2001 0689825811	pre-K–3

Title	Author	Publisher/Year ISBN	Suggested Grade Levels
Dear Baby: Letters from Your Big Brothers	Sullivan	Candlewick/2005 0763621269	K–2
The Armadillo from Amarillo	Cherry	Voyager/1994 0152019553	K–3
First Year Letters	Danneberg	Charlesbridge/2003 1580890857	K–3
Love, Lizzie: Letters to a Military Mom	McElroy	Albert Whitman/2005 0807547778	K–3

Diary Entries

Title	Author	Publisher/Year ISBN	Suggested Grade Levels
Diary of a Spider	Cronin	Joanna Cotler/2005 0060001534	pre-K–3
Diary of a Worm	Cronin	Joanna Cotler/2003 006000150X	pre-K–3

Newspaper Features

Title	Author	Publisher/Year ISBN	Suggested Grade Levels
The Nutty News	Barrett	Knopf/2005 037582751X	K–6

Labels and Signs

Title	Author	Publisher/Year ISBN	Suggested Grade Levels
Reading Makes You Feel Good	Parr	Little, Brown/2005 0316160040	pre-K–1
Souperchicken	Auch and Auch	Holiday House/2003 0823417042	K–2
Home	Baker	Greenwillow/2004 0066239354	K–3

Other Texts

Title	Author	Publisher/Year ISBN	Suggested Grade Levels
Fortune Cookie Fortunes	Linn	Knopf/2004 037581521X	pre-K–3
Max's Logbook	Moss	Scholastic/2003 0439466601	3–5
Sienna's Scrapbook	Parker	Chronicle/2005 0811843009	3–5

Sample Real-Life Materials

Environmental Print

billboards
signs
bumper stickers
buttons
T-shirts, sweatshirts, and hats

Coping with Time

bus, train, and plane schedules
TV guides
calendars
diaries
date books

Coping with Space

mailings
maps and directions
catalogs
phonebooks
letters and postcards

Coping with Complexities

labels
directions

manuals
menus
applications
coupons
advertisements
brochures

Building Community

logos
slogans
banners
balloons
cards
games

Conclusions

Even when a student has limited access to books, newspapers, and magazines, he or she still lives in a world surrounded by other real-life texts. To not make links between these texts and what happens in classroom literacy programs seems unfortunate. Clearly these texts are the best tools to engage some of our hardest-to-reach readers and to expand the reading habits of some of our best readers. They provide real-life examples of formats and structures often overlooked in other instructional materials, lending themselves to use in demonstrations during shared reading lessons. They can be used to enhance the classroom environment and become springboards for engaging independent activities. These texts are readily available at relatively no cost. What better resource to use to help students make connections between learning and life?

Anthologies

So beginning in the late 1920s, William Gray began to build the world of Dick and Jane, featuring characters by a reading consultant named Zerna Sharp, for the educational publisher Scott Foresman and Company. What Gray and Sharp and teams of passionate educators, writers, illustrators and editors produced was the map for the classic book series that taught eighty-five million children how to read from the 1930s to the 1960s.

—Carole Kismaric and Marrin Heiferman, *Growing Up with Dick and Jane*

[The basal reader] may continue to wield its power for fifteen years or fifty years, but in time it will march silently out of the classroom and be relegated to the dusty attic.

—Nila Banton Smith, *American Reading Instruction*

A Brief Description

More than seventy years have passed since Nila Banton Smith's prediction, and basal readers are still here (Roser, Hoffman, and Carr 2003). Dick and Jane may have been moved to the dusty attic, but the basal reader anthology is still on most classroom shelves and in most student desks. The anthology is the central component of a basal reading series—a collection of materials that are designed with an instructional focus in mind to become the central resource for a classroom, school, or district reading program. Long gone are days of recurring characters in repeated stories of their lives. Today the anthology is a collection of texts, many of which are complete existing fiction, nonfiction, and poetry texts or excerpts from these works. Each anthology is geared to a suggested grade level and is developed to address a list of specific strategies and skills. The anthology is often supported by additional supplemental materials, including trade books and leveled readers. Additional materials are available to support instruction based on the anthology. Basal reading systems have become so sophisticated that one company's offerings for the grade six level included more than 130 separate purchasable components, including materials for assessment, technology, and second language learners.

Why Use Them?

The most obvious reason to use selections from anthologies is their availability. Historically, more than 90 percent of classrooms relied on basal readers for reading instruction. This number has eroded somewhat as concerns about the overreliance on basal readers have been voiced over the past two decades (National Council of Teachers of English 1989). After a period of allowing teachers more choice in their selection of reading materials, however, some districts have returned to the use of a basal reading series. While the centralization of this decision has concerned some teachers, many administrators feel that it grows out of a need to foster greater continuity across and between grades within the district. Those administrators contend that a central basal allows for greater connections among teachers. It can contribute to a better sense of community within the district. More recent surveys have indicated that while relatively few teachers exclusively use basal readers, more than 80 percent still rely on basal readers to some extent in their classrooms (Baumann et al. 1998). The bottom line is that most teachers have an anthology available for use in their classroom reading programs.

We do not believe that we need to dedicate much space to providing a rationale for the traditional use of the basal anthology. Teachers probably don't need help marching through selections as they appear in the anthology while following the suggestions for instruction. We think it is more important to present a vision for the use of anthology selections that can help teachers challenge the one-size-fits-all philosophy that often surrounds the basal. In this section, let's look at why using your anthology in different ways might help you better meet the needs of the many readers in your classroom.

To Better Motivate All Readers

Since the basal reader anthology often is the text most closely identified with school reading, it may not be the best resource to motivate most readers. With the possible exception of the compliant readers who share the "My teacher says reading is important" profile in the motivational grid in Figure 1.1, the anthology probably is not the text of choice for most students. But building in choice is one way to make the anthology a bit more motivating for many students. Basal selections are often clustered around themes as units. What if, instead of assigning the same selection to all students, the teacher allowed students to choose which of the selections they would like to read? Students who are motivated by competition especially when they can succeed and those students who struggle with self-efficacy would be able to gravitate toward selections that would lead to success. Students more interested in social aspects of school life could find a selection to read and respond to together. The compliant students would have to make a choice on their own, and the reading lovers would get a bit of the choice they desire. The most difficult students to motivate still might be difficult to motivate even given some choices, but at least the other students would have their needs met better than if they had all been assigned the same selection.

To Shed Light on the Complexity of Reading

Basal reading series are often created with great attention to text factors. Large authoring and editorial teams choose selections carefully to attempt to create an anthology with content and concepts appropriate for the grade level. They spend many hours organizing the selections in formats that are reader-friendly. In the best of these materials, the purpose for the selection is clearly defined. The instructional lessons that surround the selections often focus on addressing reader factors related to the selection. The lessons assist the teacher in making sure that all readers have adequate background experiences, subject matter knowledge, and the vocabulary necessary to be successful with the texts. These lessons often show teachers how to generate interest in and excitement about the selection to help foster motivation and how to set up a clear purpose for the students' reading. Only the context factors are inherently marginalized through the use of the basal anthology. The reading almost always takes place in the school setting, where the psychological, emotional, and sociological risks can be great. Outcomes often have high stakes. It might be the context factors that unfortunately place even the best anthology in the dimmest light in the eyes of the students.

To Expand Children's Understandings of the Variety of Text Genres and Structures

In the development of the basal anthology, authoring and editorial teams often work to balance the text genres and structures included in the materials.

Historically, narrative story lines dominated the genres and structures selected for inclusion. In a 1995 edition, one thematically developed anthology focused on caring. The main texts included three fiction story excerpts (two realistic and one historical) and three nonfiction pieces (two biographies and one biographical play). The anthology also contained two poetry selections and two reflective pieces by authors about their writing. If used as suggested, this anthology would expose students to a variety of genres.

Almost all of the pieces in the section on caring, however, were organized around narrative story lines. Very few alternative text types or structures were included. Some selections were made-up stories and some were real stories, but almost all were stories. This was even more apparent in looking at the suggested and supplemental texts recommended for use with the main selections. Of the twelve texts identified for use as trade books, independent reading, read-alouds, other favorites, literature connections, and integrated curriculum, nine were fiction titles and only three were nonfiction.

More recently, publishers have worked to include more nonfiction genres and text types. In a 2001 anthology, it was easy to see these shifts. The anthology had three themes: "Tell Me a Story," "Good Neighbors," and "Celebrate Our Worlds." The first theme was almost exclusively focused on narrative story lines. Even the poem and the nonfiction selections included with this theme were based on narrative story lines. The same was true with the five recommended "Readers Choice" selections used to extend the theme beyond the anthology. With the second theme, however, the mix had shifted. The seven selections included four nonfiction pieces, and all broke from narrative story lines. They were informational texts organized in different structures—compare and contrast, main idea and supporting details, and so on. With this theme, the five "Readers Choice" recommendations included two selections based on text structures other than story lines. In the final theme, two selections were fictional (one realistic and one fantasy), one was a song, one was a poem, and three were nonfiction selections organized with main idea—supporting detail structures. For the recommended "Readers Choice" selections, only two of the five followed narrative story lines.

It is clear that basal anthologies are now being developed with attention to exposing readers to a greater variety of genres and text structures. In a newly published edition, the publishers of one basal series pointed out to those considering their materials that in the early grades there was a sixty-forty mix of fiction and nonfiction. In the middle grades that mix shifted to fifty-fifty, and in the upper grades the mix had tipped in favor of nonfiction in a forty-sixty split. Overall, this results in a fifty-fifty mix of fiction and nonfiction throughout the use of the series, but some would argue that even a fifty-fifty split results in an overemphasis on narratives in the elementary school reading program. Teachers still need to look carefully to make sure their anthology will provide an opportunity for their students to experience a wide variety of genres and text structures. Teachers must make decisions about the use of selections in their anthologies that address this concern.

To Make More Texts Acceptable and Accessible in and out of School

Anthologies might be the easiest way to make sure the same text gets into the hands of all of the readers in the classroom since copies abound in most classrooms. Since most anthologies now contain high-quality text selections, this could be the best way to guarantee that all students also have access to at least excerpts of quality literature. In addition, any single anthology contains multiple texts. You can select specific texts within the anthology to use with specific readers in the classroom. But the bottom line is that an anthology is designed for school use. The teacher is not using the anthology so that students just become better at reading basal anthologies. Students will not continue their reading habit outside of school by seeking out other anthologies. They will continue their reading habits by seeking books and other alternative texts available outside of school. Because of this, the anthology is best viewed primarily as a springboard to other texts. You must be very intentional in using basal selections to foster the acceptability of all texts in the classroom. Likewise, you must be very intentional about showing the links between basal selections and texts that are accessible outside of the classroom.

To Help Children Develop an Understanding of Intertexuality

In the past, many teachers felt the pressure to cover all of the stories in an anthology. Once one was done, it was time to move on to the next anthology. Very little effort was made to connect one story to the next, even though most current anthologies are actually organized around thematic topics. While some have criticized the selected themes as too broad and some selections as forced fits, to ignore the attempt to thematically link selections and march through them story by story without connections doesn't seem appropriate either. Again, the anthologies previously mentioned had internal organization around themes. In the 1995 anthology there were six themes: imagination, nature, Americans, what's important, caring, and growing up. The caring theme was called "Handle with Care" and was explained as "We all care! We care about what's happening in our lives, about each other and about the world around us." The anthology included six texts that all related to that theme. In the 2001 edition, the three themes each included seven main texts that were all linked. So even when the anthology doesn't explicitly suggest making connections between the texts, you should be able to find those connections and encourage your students to do so as well.

To Address the Oversimplification of Leveling Systems Often Used to Determine Which Books Children Should Read

One advantage of basal anthologies is that some time and energy has been spent to select texts that are written at the level for which the anthology was designed. In the past, selections from authentic texts were actually modified to fit readability formulas. More recently, such modifications have been minimized to honor the original language of the author. This may mean there is some variation of levels within an anthology, but generally the included texts will be within the ballpark for most of the students in that grade. Basal series often now include texts selected to provide additional challenge for those reading above grade level and appropriate practice for those reading below grade level. Because the development of these materials has included attention to levels, the teacher will not have to consume significant time and energy determining the appropriateness of the texts for students.

How Might They Be Used?

Read-aloud: Basal reading systems often contain collections of read-aloud materials that teachers can use to supplement the texts in the anthologies. Others provide suggestions of texts to use during the read-aloud period to make connections to the selections in the anthology. Selections from the anthology are also suitable read-aloud materials. In fact, teachers who feel pressure to cover the materials in the anthology but also feel the constraint of their schedule can be intentional about sharing some selections in the anthology during the read-aloud time. Many excerpts included in anthologies work quite well as read-alouds since they are shorter in length than the full piece but edited in a way that keeps the selection whole. Teachers can read one of these pieces to create excitement about the other connected texts within the anthology or to generate excitement about texts outside the anthology.

Shared reading: Selections in the anthology lend themselves very well to shared reading or whole-group activities. If you decide that a specific text needs to be in the heads of all the students in a class, the anthology makes it easy to put the same text in the hands of all children. The anthology can support a teacher-developed lesson based on the needs of the students or the demands of the local curriculum. The anthology also provides a lesson plan for using each selection that you can adopt or adapt.

Some basal reading systems provide separate materials to use for shared reading. Primary-grade teachers may have access to enlarged big books to use in large-group instructional lessons. In the intermediate grades, formats may be changed to include overhead transparencies of text excerpts. Other instructional aids like charts and posters may also be available for use in shared reading formats. These materials can be used separately by teachers to support teacher-developed lessons, but they are also often designed to help make connections between the shared reading and other aspects of a balanced reading program.

Guided reading: Fawson and Reutzel (2000) take on the frequently asked question about the connection between guided reading and basal programs in an article called "But I Only Have a Basal." They remind teachers that guided reading is more about how one uses materials than what materials one uses. Basal selections can be used in guided reading programs. The selections are already leveled. (In fact, in their article, Fawson and Reutzel identify guided reading levels for some common basal reading selections.) And if every student has an anthology, it is easy to put the selection in the hands of all students. Our national survey of guided reading practices in primary classrooms revealed that many teachers used their basal stories for guided reading in addition to "little books" and trade books.

In addition, many basal reading systems have supplemental materials for the specific purpose of serving as guided reading components of balanced literacy programs. Sets of leveled readers often accompany basal anthologies. Use caution in using separate sets of materials for guided reading within or with a basal system, though. Unless these materials can be connected in some way, many students might not transfer learning from the instruction in the anthology to the instruction done with the leveled readers.

Independent reading: Unless the basal reading system provides a library of individual titles for students to read during a recreational reading period, the anthology is probably not the best resource for this aspect of a balanced reading program. While students could sample and revisit any selections in the anthology, this time would likely be better spent working with materials that more closely look like what readers read beyond the school walls.

Using Anthologies with Younger Elementary-Aged Readers

When Kerry heard that a group of anthologies that had been retired to the central curriculum storage room were going to be discarded, she asked if she could have multiple copies before they were tossed out. She worked to remove the covers from the printed pages. She separated the pages and was able to create separate copies of *My Friends,* by Taro Gomi, *The Little Red Hen,* by Byron Barton, *Flower Garden,* by Eve Bunting, *The Very Hungry Caterpillar,* by Eric Carle, and *A Color of His Own,* by Leo Lionni. She made some simple bindings and ended up with multiple-copy sets of these five popular texts. She doubled-checked the level for each one before adding them to her guided reading titles. Once she had used them in guided reading, she placed copies of them in her leveled baskets in her first-grade classroom library for students to reread during independent practice time.

Since each title was also introduced with "Meet the Author" and/or "Meet the Illustrator" pages, she placed each of these single pages on heavy background paper and laminated them so she could add them to a collection of other materials focused on authors and illustrators that she used in workshop lessons and that the students had access to. She didn't let poems in the anthology go to waste either. There was "The Sharing Song," by Raffi, "My Mami Takes Me to the Bakery," by Charlotte Pomerantz, "Together," by Paul Engle, "My Opinion," by Monica Shannon, a haiku by Chisoku, and a poem by student Amanda Venta called "Flowers." Depending on the length of the poems, she put them on heavy paper, laminated them, and added them to a box of poems students visit for fluency practice. Finally, there were directions for a number of response activities following the main text selections: performing a puppet show, making a window box, making musical instruments (shoe-box banjo, oatmeal-box drum, humming comb), making a fishing pole, making a get-well card, and illustrating like Eric Carle. There were even directions for five projects that students could do to make a difference in the world and help others. Again, Kerry put the directions on heavy paper and laminated them, creating a set of activity cards with easy-to-read directions that she could integrate into her learning centers to independently engage her students. When she reflected on how much she had gotten out of the soon-to-be-discarded basals, she wondered whether more teachers might get more out of the anthologies if everything wasn't bound together in one big textbook.

Using Anthologies with Older Elementary-Aged Readers

In Anna's building, all teachers had access to basal reading materials but the focus was always on achieving identified outcomes for the fifth-grade level. Each teacher was allowed to develop his or her reading program flexibly as long as the teacher could demonstrate that students had made progress toward the identified outcomes. Anna developed her reading program around the use of a variety of reading and writing materials that included but was not limited to her anthology and the basal reading series.

Anna liked to thematically link the focus of her reading and writing materials and activities for short periods of time. One of the anthology themes that she really liked was a unit on caring. She felt it was important to help her students move toward being concerned about others. This helped set a more positive tone within the classroom and extended her influence in the lives of her students beyond the classroom.

Anna started the unit with a whole-class selection from the anthology. It was an excerpt called "Jessi's Secret Language," by Ann Martin, from one of the books in the Baby-Sitters Club series. It focused on gaining insights about hearing-impaired individuals. The excerpt was accessible for most of her students, especially when provided additional support in the large-group setting. It also linked to the independent reading that some students were doing with the other books in this series.

Once this excerpt was in the heads of all of her students, Anna opened up the choice for students to continue to read on this theme. She made her students aware of the other excerpts in the anthologies that related to the theme. The anthology selections represented both fiction and non-fiction texts, most of which were accessible for her students. Two excerpts were by Lois Lowry. One was from *Number the Stars*, but Anna made sure that students who needed an additional challenge also had access to a set of texts that included the full novel and other related titles suggested by the basal, like Betsy Byar's *Pinballs* (1977). She also allowed them to select a book outside of the anthology as long as they could link it to the caring theme.

Anna also was able to use two anthology selections as part of the independent work she identified as options for projects for her students to work on during the theme. One was a biographical play by Glenette Tilley Turner called "Meet the Inventor of the Stoplight." She formed a team of interested students who would perform the play as a readers' theatre selection with minimal props and settings. She liked how the play would provide a genuine reason for students to repeatedly practice their reading, improving their fluency and building their comfort and confidence along the way. The other was a defined project called "At Your Service" that focused on the development of a directory of community resources. Students would compile available resources to build a directory they could publish and share with others. This directory would contain information on where community members could go for help and support to address common needs in the area. Anna loved how the project forced her students to become familiar with and use real-life texts, from telephone directories to informational pamphlets from local organizations. It encouraged her students to explore the Internet in a focused, serious way to get more information about local resources that could help other individuals.

In the end even though Anna had not marched through the anthology selection by selection, she knew that her students had explored most of the anthology texts as well as many others. She knew that using her anthology as a resource and building in more choice and flexibility helped her students not only accomplish the outcomes for the unit but go beyond them as well.

Sample Titles

Basically there are four key companies producing five basal anthologies. Different editions have different brand names, but each is often known by its publisher:

Harcourt Trophies: www.harcourtschool.com/menus/reading.html
Houghton Mifflin Reading: www.eduplace.com/rdg/hmr06 (Education Place support website)
Macmillan/McGraw Hill Reading: www.macmillanmh.com/reading /2005/teacher/teachres
Open Court Reading (McGraw Hill): www.sraonline.com/index.php /home/curriculumsolutions/reading/ocr/622
Scott Foresman Reading Street (Pearson): www.scottforesman.com /tours/reading/index.cfm

Conclusions

Dick and Jane have made a bit of a comeback lately. The original readers have been reissued and are available for purchase in catalogs of retro items. Dick and Jane now don calendars, book bags, and kitchen magnets. Michael Ford even found a display of Dick and Jane activity books at the end of an aisle in his local grocery store. Perhaps it is just a marketing trend capturing boomers as they wax nostalgic for old, familiar friends? But it serves as another reminder that no matter the concerns voiced about basal readers, this billion-dollar industry is not disappearing. While the number of teachers using anthologies may change over the years, most will have access to these texts in their classrooms. So in a book focused on the use of alternative texts in classroom reading programs, why devote any space to the use of the one text that has almost always been in every classroom? We thought it was important to remind everyone that often it is not the text being used, but *how* the text is being used that matters. Remember that any of the alternative texts that we have discussed in this book can be used in a way that fails to address any or all of the goals we have identified for using those texts in the first place. On the other hand, there are traditional texts that can be used in creative ways so that they do address those goals. That is why we decided to take a second look at basal readers in this chapter. What have we discovered? Many teachers have access to these materials. By building some flexibility into their instructional use of these materials, teachers may discover that they can use the advantages of the anthologies (accessibility, structure, instructional ideas) to help address issues like motivation, exposure to a variety of texts and structures, appropriateness of levels, and intertextuality. Clearly, the creative teacher can find ways to integrate the use of an anthology with other texts in addressing the needs of the many different readers in his classroom.

11

Cyber Texts

Gis Igne's ypm Gxliqy.
H$'s sssli3g a zqcht c+@12d
#wMqo zmi 0jr.

The message on the computer screen is nonsense. But it's the last message
Josh Allan, Rob Zanelli and Tamsyn Smith receive over the internet from a
yachtsman alone at sea—and they're sure it contains a clue to the identity
of an international art thief. Now they must decipher the scrambled
message and with time running out, set a trap for a dangerous enemy.

—Michael Coleman, *Internet Detectives: Speed Surf*

Students need to be taught to read electronic texts in addition to the
conventional texts they already learn to read. The amount of electronic and
multimedia text is expanding exponentially, and our students need to be
able to deal with it if they are to be literate in the modern world. Both
types of electronic text should be present and be used in instruction in
classrooms of today to prepare our students for tomorrow.

—Michael L. Kamil, Helen S. Kim, and Diane M. Lane,
"Electronic Text in the Classroom"

A Brief Description

Cyber texts are any texts that exist in electronic digital environments. These
texts are primarily accessible through computers and available on the

Internet. The increasing proliferation of handheld devices and wireless accessibility means that cyber texts now can be received and composed virtually anywhere, any time, by any one. While almost any text in cyberspace can be downloaded and read in a printed format, for this chapter we are focusing on texts that are actually read in the digital environments. Kamil, Kim, and Lane (2004) classify electronic text in two primary categories. First is any text found on the computer screen (email messages, help screens, instructions). They point out that this text exists digitally and can be transmitted from one computer to another. Except for navigational differences, readers often approach this text in a way similar to how they approach print formats. The second category is any electronic text augmented by hyperlinks, hypertext, or hypermedia. These augmented texts are more complicated texts most often found on the Internet. Reading augmented texts leads to reading experiences that are quite different from those gained when reading traditional print formats.

Why Use Them?

Some people don't even call the students we teach the *next* generation; they call them the *net* generation. In his award-winning young adult novel *Feed,* M. T. Anderson (2004) actually imagines a time when an Internet-television hybrid is implanted in people's brains at birth. Text messages are sent and received without external technology. School actually is a copyrighted piece of software. While his world does not quite reflect what is happening today, it is quite clear that this generation operates within a cyber world and reading habits have changed. Research projects that would have taken a student to the library now begin online at home on a personal computer. This trend will only accelerate as the technology becomes even more accessible, affordable, and usable. In fact, the cyber texts that we define today may not be the same cyber texts we'll be talking about tomorrow (IRA 2001). In their book *Innovative Approaches to Literacy Education: Using the Internet to Support New Literacies* (Karchmer et al. 2005), Leu et al. (2005) observe that new literacies are continuously emerging to meet the demands of an ever growing set of information and communication technologies. Leu et al. define new literacies as

> the skills, strategies, and dispositions necessary to successfully use and adapt to the rapidly changing information and communication technologies and contexts that continuously emerge in our world and influence all areas of our personal and professional lives. These new literacies allow

us to use the internet and other information and communication technology to identify important problems, locate information, analyze the usefulness of that information, synthesize information to solve problems, and communicate the solutions to others. (2004, 1572)

If students are going to operate in this cyber world, it makes sense to provide them with the strategies they will need to be successful. Beginning with the five strategies Leu and his colleagues (Karchmer et al. 2005) identify is a good first step in helping students meet the technological demands that exist with cyber texts today:

- constructing and comprehending information on the Internet
- using search engines to find information
- critically evaluating information found on the Web
- sending messages
- using word processors

In light of these technological demands, we need to expand our definition of what it means to be literate, to rethink what it means to be a reader, and to reevaluate what we consider appropriate texts for classrooms (Coiro 2003; McKenna, Labbo, and Reinking 2003). For example, being literate now includes being able to sort quality websites from the many sites suggested by a search engine. In Google's newsletter for librarians (see www .google.com/newsletter/librarian/librarian_2005_12/newsletter.html), the authors list five characteristics to help readers find websites they can trust (see Figure 11.1).

Clearly, cyber text calls on readers to use new literacies that transcend traditional texts (Coiro 2003). Readers must do more than skim or study texts. They must "adopt a more critical stance toward texts or risk being unknowingly tricked, persuaded, or biased" (461). Helping students learn and apply new literacies so that they can be successful readers in every sense of the term, then, is the most important reason for using cyber text. Let's look at other reasons for including cyber texts on the menu of acceptable and valued texts in a classroom reading program.

To Better Motivate All Readers

For those readers who are the most difficult to motivate, cyber texts have three distinct advantages. First, cyber texts are often perceived as something

Characteristic	Questions to Determine Trustworthiness
Availability	Is the site up and running? Is the information freely available?
Credibility	Does the site contribute current, accurate information? Is the site author qualified to present the content?
Authorship	Is it free from typographical and grammatical errors?
External links	Is it free from broken links?
Legality	Is it created within copyright and fair-use guidelines?

totally removed from the school reading materials with which these children have not had much success. Instead of reminding them of the texts they have struggled with, cyber texts are seen by these students as attractive, something new and different. Second, cyber texts provide the possibility of finding something at an appropriate difficulty level that isn't in an inappropriate format. Instead of handing an older struggling reader a picture book with text at his or her level, teachers can search the Net for texts at the reader's level in a format that doesn't have any stigma attached to it. Finally, cyber texts exist on an endless number of topics (Leu 2002). Teachers should be able to find more than one topic they can use to entice their most difficult-to-reach readers.

Cyber texts also have motivational qualities for other student profiles. For example, cyber texts have a strong appeal to those students more interested in social relationships (Solomon 2002; El-Hindi 1998). In fact, the editors of a recent church bulletin recommend that families check out what their teenagers might be writing and reading on social networking websites, including MySpace.com. This is a site where hundreds of thousands of computer users electronically drop in daily to leave their thoughts and ideas in response to others' thoughts and ideas that they have read on the site. MySpace.com has an estimated 70 million users and is the second most viewed website in the United States. Recent discussions focused on how MySpace.com can be made more compatible for handheld devices and how certain devices may be dedicated for this purpose. While the most popular, it is the not the only site where students can share their own writing and invite responses. Student Online Publishing (www.emtech.net/student_

publishing.htm) is another. Since one of the primary functions of cyber texts is to help us communicate with one another over space and time, we need to capitalize on them to motivate the reading and writing of those students who usually steer clear of reading and writing.

Students who lack a high degree of self-efficacy may find a greater level of comfort and ease when working with cyber text, thus boosting their self-efficacy. Surfing the Net, for instance, is sure to increase students' confidence and competence, enabling them to see themselves as increasingly better readers. Indeed, Solomon (2002) reports increased self-efficacy and attitude toward learning when students work collaboratively. Using an Internet workshop (Leu 2002) in which children visit different websites related to the same topic and share their findings is one example of this collaboration.

As valuable as cyber text is, a word of caution is in order here. There are many different types of cyber texts, including computer-based reading programs, which don't appeal to all students. For example, there are commercial computerized programs that engage students in goal setting and reward students with points and prizes for successfully reaching those goals by completing online tests about texts. These programs might appeal to some students, but to assume they will motivate all students ignores the complexity of motivation that we discuss in this book. If using these programs motivates those who are already voracious readers and does little to engage those who need to be motivated the most, they are not fulfilling the original intent for using them.

To Shed Light on the Complexity of Reading

There are differences between reading a screen and reading a page (Coiro 2003). These text factors can complicate reading for some. Kamil and Lane (1998) argue that reading onscreen is 15 to 20 percent less efficient than reading hard copy. Some of the inefficiency is due to issues related to screen resolution. Texts on screen can be less clear than print on a page. Part of the inefficiency is also due to the increased need for navigational skills. Screens often hold less text and require more navigation than the traditional page. Perhaps this is why many readers still prefer downloading and printing text and reading it in hard copy rather than on the screen.

On the other hand, cyber texts also have features that can make reading easier for readers. The text is easily searchable; the computer can scan and skim more effectively than a reader can. It is easily modified. Software exists to reformat cyber texts into more viewer-friendly formats for different purposes (McKenna, Labbo, and Reinking 2003; Leu et al. 2004). It is easily transportable. Huge volumes of cyber texts can be reduced to a single CD or flash drive and easily transported to another computer.

Electronic texts with hypermedia links actually can provide support for comprehension (Coiro 2003). Imagine not understanding a word, concept, or idea you are reading about and then being able to click on the screen to get more information about it. The photo or video that comes up will provide the clarification you need to better understand the passage. This cross-checking is an example of one of the unique strategies that many children need to be taught in order to successfully read cyber texts (McKenna, Labbo, and Reinking 2003).

Given that the Internet adds to the complexity of reading by requiring readers to use new literacies, readers with limited background knowledge and experience need to begin in more restrictive electronic environments where the choices aren't too overwhelming. For younger readers, you might provide specific websites for students to visit and teach them the specific new literacy skill(s) they need in order to navigate the site independently. As when introducing students to any new skill, we also need to explicitly teach students what is important when visiting websites, especially when they are linked to other texts and media. Otherwise these built-in supports become distractions that actually could interfere with the reader's ability to understand a cyber text.

To Expand Children's Understandings of the Variety of Text Genres and Structures

Because almost any text that exists in print format may be found on the Web, cyber texts can be used to expose students to a variety of traditional genres and structures. For example, the Children's Literature Web Guide, www.acs .ucalgary.ca/~dkbrown, provides readers with full-length novels. Informative prose dominates web pages, however. Descriptive and procedural nonfiction texts define the structures of most of the texts. While narrative prose is available on the Net, one survey revealed that 95 percent of a random sample of web pages contained information text (Kamil and Lane 1998).

Cyber text can also be a genre of its own, combining a number of genres to create a unique structure (Chandler-Olcott and Mahar 2001). For example, in his series Internet Detectives, Michael Coleman integrates features from cyber text in his traditional novels. He uses replications of computer screens containing email messages and web pages to present these high-tech mysteries.

Another point to consider is that digital literacy (e.g., websites, chat rooms, instant messaging, and list servers) can be viewed as a genre in and of itself. According to Harris and Hodges, one definition of genre is "any type of discourse that possesses typified, distinguishable conventions of form, style, or content in recurring contexts" (1995, 96). Therefore, Chandler-Olcott and Mahar (2001) note that each type of digital literacy can be considered a genre. Consequently, they suggest integrating digital texts into genre study so that students will more fully understand *genre*.

Coiro (2003) explains that the Internet offers students new text formats and that using these formats gives students and teachers alike a broader view of *text*. Nonlinear, interactive, and multimedia forms are three types of web-based texts. Her point echoes ours: Children more fully develop an understanding of cyber text structures by engaging with them. They also learn how to use new literacies to best comprehend the text.

To Make More Texts Acceptable and Accessible in and out of School

In a column on issues and trends on literacy, Malloy and Gambrell (2006) take on the "unavoidable"—literacy instruction and the Internet. Malloy and Gambrell point out that what was once primarily a resource, tool, and forum for teens and adults is now negotiated frequently and with relative ease by younger students as well. Like other aspects of their literate lives, many of these students have learned how to do this with very little explicit instruction, especially in school reading programs. It is clear that the self-initiated reading of cyber texts outside of school reading programs is done for both recreational and instructional purposes. Malloy and Gambrell conclude: "It is our job as teachers to understand and appreciate the unavoidable and prepare for it" (492). Kamil and his colleagues agree: "In the future, no student (or adult) will be able to avoid electronic text or multimedia information" (2004, 161). To their reasoning, we add that using cyber texts for a variety of instructional purposes signals acceptance to students.

As important as acceptance is accessibility. We often take for granted that which we have and this is certainly true when we think of computers and access to the Internet. Our own sons, for example, have always had access to computers and the Internet at home. The same is not true for all children. Some have computers but no Internet access. Others have neither. Making both accessible in school becomes critical if we truly want to help all students function in our technological society.

Beyond the concrete part of accessibility, though, is the issue of making cyber text accessible for students who struggle with reading and, as a result, struggle for acceptance from classmates (Cohen 1994). Recognizing that these students often need a morale boost, Leu et al. (2004) suggest that we can deliberately make them the experts on a new literacy (e.g., using the cursor to point to individual words) by teaching it to them first. These students can then teach others the same skill. The result is that children begin to see that they are a community of learners and, as such, can learn much from one another, regardless of perceived reading level. The New Literacies website (http://ctell.uconn.edu/cases/newliteracies.htm) provides a live example of how a second-grade teacher uses this particular strategy. McKenna, Labbo, and Reinking (2003) offer two additional examples by explaining how a kindergarten teacher and a first-grade teacher use cyber texts as a part of their reading and writing instruction.

Let's also remember learning styles when we think of accessibility! Some cyber texts offer additional help for children who need physical support for one reason or another. Some children, for example, rely on their auditory processes, and audio recordings found in many cyber texts enable them to receive this support. Starfall's website (http://starfall.com) provides several texts for students to read with auditory and visual support. For example, when students read "The Gingerbread Man," they can listen to a recording of each word. Each word is also highlighted, thus enabling children to see word boundaries. Finally, at the end of this version of the story, the gingerbread man runs on the screen as the final lines are played. And last, students are given an opportunity to evaluate whether or not they liked the story by clicking on one of three faces used to denote happy, neutral, or unhappy.

To Help Children Develop an Understanding of Intertexuality

Cyber texts are often deliberately connected with links from one text to another. Therefore, the intertextual connections that a reader of print materials needs to make internally without assistance are often made available to the reader in cyber texts. Electronic texts, for instance, are built with hyperlinks that take readers right to another related text. If readers have acquired the requisite new literacy(ies) necessary to navigate such a website, they merely need to click on identified links to move from one text to another. More explanation or information about a reference made in one text is easily accessed by a click of the mouse. The nonlinear nature of reading online is often a recursive process of moving from one connected text to another.

Hypermedia actually builds in links from electronic texts to other media, which enhances intertexual connections.

Readers also make intertextual connections when they explore the same topic but visit different websites. For example, children might be learning about hurricanes and, in an open-ended assignment, be directed to visit at least one website that has information about hurricanes, write out at least three ideas from the site, and then discuss findings with other students. Students not only exchange information about hurricanes but also exchange information about their websites. Doing so better helps readers to understand that there is a tremendous amount of information that can be retrieved and evaluated for accuracy on the Internet. They also begin to see how to use many sources to validate findings.

To Address the Oversimplification of Leveling Systems Often Used to Determine Which Books Children Should Read

The wide variety of cyber texts ensures that texts exist on the Web at all levels. Kamil and Lane (1998) found, however, the average readability level in their random sample of web pages to be around tenth grade. In fact, when they looked specifically at pages designed by teachers for students, the average readability was only slightly lower (a grade level of 9.3). This often means that many students are being exposed to cyber texts that are too difficult for them. The key—whether the reader is reading on the Web or the page—is making sure that the texts being read are appropriate for the learners reading them. In other words, just because students surf the Net doesn't necessarily mean they will automatically find material that is the right difficulty level and/or has appropriate content.

Fortunately, there are ways that we can help children select cyber texts they can read. For example, we can visit websites ourselves with our students in mind and make a list of those that will ensure reading success. We can also permit students to select their own websites and, as with traditional print, have them evaluate the difficulty of the text for themselves. We can encourage them to use the five-finger rule, in which they raise a finger for each word that poses difficulty. If all fingers on a hand are used within the first page, they should get out of that site and try another.

All of the above being said, some words of caution are in order here. First, we need to be mindful that because of their design, many cyber texts defy leveling as we know it in the traditional printed-text world. Some cyber texts have accompanying read-aloud voices, making it possible for students of varying levels to engage with texts that might be beyond their reading level in terms of ability to identify words. Others provide assistance by highlighting words and speaking the words as students point the cursor at them. As a result, students increase their store of sight vocabulary (McKenna, Reinking, and Labbo 1997) and thus their reading levels. Texts such as these, then, serve as literacy scaffolds, enabling students to accelerate their reading growth.

A second point we wish to underscore is that as with other texts, readers bring their own interests and backgrounds to cyber texts. As a result, they are often able to read text that may be beyond their perceived levels according to their performances on a reading test.

Third, reading is more than calling words. Therefore, we need to permit students to read cyber texts that may be beneath their perceived levels depending on their purpose for reading. For example, students might choose to read a cyber text for enjoyment during independent reading. Easy-to-read text is a perfect fit because students can focus on enjoying the text rather than on decoding or encountering unknown words. At other times, students might be searching for information about an animal or some other topic. Because the information seeking is driving the reading, their reading level takes a backseat. It matters not if students obtain the information from a site that they can read with ease or one that is challenging.

How Might They Be Used?

Read-aloud: Other texts would probably be better sources of read-aloud material than cyber texts. Certainly anything could be downloaded and read aloud to students, but to actually read aloud from the Web is not likely to be the most efficient way to use read-aloud time. With the right projection equipment, a teacher could share a cyber text with the class and read it aloud. Under those circumstances it might be very difficult, however, to capture the more intimate magic of a read-aloud time where children are gathered around a teacher reading aloud from a book.

Shared reading: Shared reading is a time when we gather students together to share a text with a specific teaching point in mind. Many times teachers use books large enough for all to see (i.e., big books). With the right projection equipment, cyber texts are a perfect fit. For example, if you are trying to help students understand speech-to-print matching, you can call up any number of stories from a website such as Starfall.com. After reading the story through for enjoyment, you can return to it using the cursor to point to every word as you read. Because words are highlighted as you point to them, students experience speech-to-print matching.

Guided reading: One of the luxuries of small-group guided reading is that it affords us with opportunities to work with a small number of students. As with any instruction that carries the guided reading label, though, we have to first think of why we are calling the group of students together in the first place. That is, what is it that this particular group of students needs to learn? As it pertains to learning new literacy skills, the answer to this question might be to help students understand how to click on different hyperlinks embedded within a website such as The Rainforest (www.christiananswers .net/kids/rainforest/home.htm), which provides information about rain forests. Once the group is gathered around the computer, we can first model the process by accessing the website. We can then invite students to talk about what they see on the opening page and what they would like to read about first. We can then place the cursor on that particular topic, clicking while we are talking. Students can then read what appears on the screen, or we can read it to them. We can then provide students with practice by returning to the home page and having them click on another topic. True, this demonstration stretches the notion of guided reading beyond helping students read text and includes helping students acquire new literacies. While the ideal would be to have each student equipped with a laptop, the modification we provide here is still a workable and doable option for guided reading. Some shareware (software that allows small groups to work on the same text) would allow some guided reading and writing instruction mediated by the teacher, but this can happen only if classrooms are equipped with the necessary technology.

Independent reading: Independent reading offers many opportunities for students to read cyber text. In another publication, we discuss the importance of meaningfully engaging students who are working independently (Ford and Opitz 2002). Reading cyber text is a perfect example. Students can independently (or with a partner) locate information related to a specific topic with the expectation that they will then share their findings with others. At other times, with a recreational focus, students can visit preapproved websites of their choosing and read about topics of interest. With an instructional focus, cyber texts can be the resources students independently consult as they work on research and inquiry projects. The Internet workshop (Leu 2002) is a fitting example. Leu suggests these four procedures for creating an Internet workshop activity:

1. Locate an appropriate site and set a bookmark for the location. You might consider visiting *Ask for Kids,* which is a directory and a search engine. Type in your question and it will find you the site that best answers the question.

2. Design the activity making sure that students need to use the site to complete it.

3. Provide students with time to complete the activity.

4. Provide time for students to share their discoveries.

Leu notes that once students are familiar with this format, they can then conduct their own inquiry projects.

These are but a few ways that students can meaningfully engage with cyber texts during independent reading.

Using Cyber Texts with Younger Elementary-Aged Readers

Kamil, Kim, and Lane (2004) present a vision of how instructional technology can be gradually introduced to young children. While accounting for developmental differences between the primary grades, they describe how creating cyber texts can support literacy instruction. They began in a kindergarten classroom where classroom helpers introduced children to the computer through the use of simple software packages designed for young students. Once the students had become comfortable with the computers, the teacher worked with a technology and media specialist to gather resources related to the content themes used to organize instruction in the classroom. These resources included appropriate cyber texts. In one case, the content focused on habitats. The teacher began the theme by sharing information with the whole group. Students were engaged in talking about the subject and what they had learned. With the help of the technology specialist, the students used Kid Pix to copy their writing and drawings about habitats on the computer, creating a collective slide show about what they had learned about the topic. The cyber text they created was then converted to a hard-copy version so students could also read it that way.

In first grade the expectations were raised a bit. Students began the year collaborating on a project. They were introduced to the use of a digital camera and learned how to integrate photos with their writing on Kid Pix. They borrowed the structure of Eric Carle's book *Have You Seen My Cat?* to create their book *Have You Seen My Principal?* using the digital photos they had taken while interviewing people in their school building. After these collaborative experiences, gradually groups or individual students began creating short slide shows and cyber texts on their own. By second grade, students pursued and assembled their own resources as they completed inquiry projects on countries in Europe. Planning and creating cyber texts were done with even less teacher support.

In this school, there was an intentional gradual release of responsibility for using and creating cyber texts as students moved through the grades. Expectations were raised to developmentally appropriate levels as students became increasingly more competent with their literacy and technology skills and strategies.

Using Cyber Texts with Older Elementary-Aged Readers

Mary Kreul (2005) moved to a fourth-grade classroom that contained her previous students from second grade. Because of her previous focus on technology, many of these students were already competent with using software to create cyber texts. The first thing she noticed with the fourth graders was her ability to train a few students to use new software and hardware and then rely on them to train other students. Students became resources for each other, allowing Mary time to provide support where it was needed most. Students began to operate efficiently in cyberspace. The writing process flowed more smoothly with pervasive use of word processing for drafting and revising work. Book reports were replaced with book reviews that were organized and added to a class website. Labeled book reviews by kids for kids were available for others to consult and discuss in selecting new texts to read. A field trip to a restored stagecoach inn, the Wade House, became the catalyst for Wisconsin history projects, in which students imagined citizens who might have lived in Wisconsin in the 1860s. These projects involved online research. Resulting essays and portraits were prepared as online products and posted on the class website for public viewing. Students responded to comments posted by others after reviewing the reports. This experience led to a similar project focused on real Wisconsin citizens. Students prepared nonfiction reports on famous Wisconsinites that were also made publicly available on the class website.

Mary also involved her class in a number of tele-collaborative Internet projects that connected her class to other classes around the United States and the world. These included "Postcard Geography," organized by Leni Dolan, through which classes exchanged local postcards with partner classes around the country, and "You Are My Hero: A 9/11 Remembrance Project," sponsored by Harriet Stolzenberg, which involved identifying, describing, and sharing heroes in their lives with others throughout the country. Mary even involved her class in tele-collaborative literature circles, working with a class of first-grade students and preservice teachers. Each group read and responded to books like *Pippi Longstocking* and then worked on a variety of collaborative projects posted on linked websites for each group to enjoy.

Sample Titles That Involve the Use of Cyber Texts

Title	Author	Publisher/Year ISBN	Suggested Grade Levels
Internet Detectives: Speed Surf	Coleman	Skylark/1997 0553486225	3–5
Feed	Anderson	Candlewick/2004 0763622591	6–8
ttfn	Myracle	Amulet/2006 0810959712	9–10
ttyl	Myracle	Harry Abrams/2005 0810987880	9–10

Conclusions

We agree with the other experts we cite in this chapter; the literate lives of our students currently involve cyber texts. Their future involvement with those texts will become more intense, not less. Leu and his colleagues (2005) observe that in the next few years, nearly every employee will be using the Internet at work. Sixty percent of all households already have Internet access, and the number of households with access doubles each year. The unique features of cyber texts will demand new literacies, some of which we don't even know about, as information and communication technologies continue to emerge. Now that almost 90 percent of all classrooms have Internet access (National Center for Education Statistics 2003), it would seem silly to deny these texts a place in the classroom reading program. To do so would limit our ability to meet the needs of the many different readers in that classroom. By not addressing these new literacies, we are assuming that students will acquire them on their own. This is a faulty assumption that may prevent some students from gaining the strategies they'll need to function in and outside of school. Rather than taking this risk, let's play an active role in helping all students acquire and develop new literacies.

Sample Websites

In addition to the websites cited throughout this chapter, we offer the following five sites, which are primarily designed for children.

Yahooligans! (http://yahooligans.yahoo.com) is a web guide for children. As a search engine, it searches for specific information that students request.

Children's Reading Room (http://unmuseum.mus.pa.us/crr) contains a selection of stories that children can download and print for their reading. Stories vary in length.

PBS Kids (http://pbskids.org) features sites for Arthur, Barney, and Clifford, among many other children's characters. Children can access stories, games, music, and even coloring forms related to different characters.

Children's Storybooks Online: Stories for Kids of All Ages (www.magickeys.com/books) offers free storybooks for young and older children and young adults. Many of the books are illustrated. The site also features riddles, puzzles, and information about how to publish a book.

RIF Reading Planet (http://rif.org/readingplanet) is run by Reading Is Fundamental. This site features, among other activities, a story maker that enables children to personalize stories by using their own words to add to a story. Children can also replace some words in the story and can write their own endings.

CHAPTER 12

The Last Part First

Virginia shuts her car door and walks toward the school entrance. It is February and it is well into the school year. She is always one of the first teachers to arrive, so before opening the school door, she reaches down and picks up the pile of newspapers that her class subscribes to. She remembers it is Thursday, the day the kids page will be in the paper, and it will be the next installment of the Breakfast Serials that Avi is writing. Her students will be excited to read the new chapter.

When she goes into the office to grab her mail, she greets the secretaries. Virginia reaches into her mailbox and pulls out the *Time for Kids* magazines that she's ordered. She struggles a bit as she carries the newspapers and the magazines down to her room. As she walks, she checks out the cover of *Time for Kids*. She sees it's about the winter Olympics in Italy. *Oh, beautiful,* she thinks to herself. *This will tie in wonderfully with the new Tacky the Penguin book the class is reading,* Tacky and the Winter Games *(Lester 2005). I hope students make that connection.*

She unlocks her door and turns on the lights. She sets her load down on the table in the front of the room. *I'd better change the daily poem before I forget,* she tells herself. She walks over to the calendar area and flips the chart-paper holder to the Arnold Adoff poem "Inspiration: Chocolate" (1989). She wonders to herself if anyone but her will see the connection between Valentine's Day chocolates and the poem. She hopes the children will.

When the morning bell rings, Virginia's students all come running into the room. She notices that two of her students, Peter and Andrew, are holding books as they walk in, and they are talking very animatedly. This surprises her because they both are reluctant and resistant readers. She smiles as she sees that Peter is reading a joke book, and Andrew is bringing back a

161

Calvin and Hobbes anthology. She is glad that she ordered those books and put them on her shelves.

"I found one, I found one!" her student Heather comments, running up to Virginia as she enters the room. "I found the bumper sticker I was telling you about last week," Heather tells Virginia excitedly. She holds out a bumper sticker that reads, "Be Patriotic: Vote Bush Out." *Well, this should lead to a good discussion,* Virginia thinks, chuckling to herself.

"Go ahead and put it up on the kiosk, Heather," she tells her student. She points to a large cardboard tube that she obtained from a carpet warehouse. She built a base so that she could stand it upright in one corner of her classroom. With some simple decorations, the kiosk is now an easy place for her students to post their signs, announcements, photos, notes, and a growing section of bumper stickers. She continues, "That will be great for our discussion during reading time."

Virginia's students find their way to the corner, where an old overstuffed chair anchors the reading area. She opens the day by asking all her students to stand up. She quickly flashes cards with names on them. Students sit down as soon as they see their name go by, and all discover quickly that Mac and Abby are absent today. She hands their cards to the attendance taker, who fills out the attendance slip and posts it outside the room. She grabs the poetry book *Lunch Money and Other Poems About School,* by Carol Diggory Shields (1998), and reads a new poem, "Eddie Edwards," aloud to her students. They ask her to read it again and join her in filling in words and phrases from the poem. They reread a few more old favorites, like "After School" from Shields' other anthology, *Almost Late for School: And More School Poems* (2003). She leaves the poem books out and invites the students to try reading them on their own. The books join a growing collection of titles proudly displayed on the tray of the class whiteboard at the front of the room.

She reaches into the class song sock and draws out a song title from the long, white decorated tube sock. Since it is an old favorite, "Ten in a Bed," they quickly sing it together, adding actions along the way. She reminds the students that they have a book based on the song and they can find it and others like it in the "Read a Song, Sing a Book" tub in the library area. After singing, they settle in for a few minutes of sharing. Two students have brought in a special section of the local newspaper previewing the upcoming Olympics. Another has brought in travel brochures from her aunt's recent trip to Italy. Virginia puts all the materials related to the Olympics in a special theme tub and reminds the students they can explore these materials during independent reading time.

That seems to be the perfect transition for her shared reading lesson. She uses her name cards to quickly dismiss the students from the carpet back to their desks. She has created overheads from a two-page article on snow-boarding in *Boys' Life* that she will use to set the stage for reading and writing about winter Olympic sports and events. First, she grabs a blank transparency and invites her students to turn to a blank page in their learning logs. She creates a web with *Olympic sport* in the middle circle and spokes going out to each side. She asks her students to help her think about what they would expect to learn if they were reading about an Olympic sport. As questions surface, she writes the ideas down on each spoke—*What is it? Who does it? How is it done? Where is it done? How do you train for it?*— and invites her students to create the same web in their learning logs. She then puts the article on snowboarding on the overhead. She begins reading the first part of the article out loud. She pauses after the first section and uses a think-aloud to show the students how to record information they have just learned on the webs they created. She invites the class to chorally read the next section of the article with her. She has her students tell her what they have learned that now could be added to the webs. Next she asks her students to finish up the reading on the screen and add to their webs on their own. She then has her students share with each other as buddies before surfacing some more details in a final large-group discussion. She links the lesson to the reading project they will be working on while she meets with small groups. She rolls in a cart filled with materials about winter Olympic sports and invites them to select a sport or event and begin to read and find out as much as they can about their sport, keeping track of their notes on a new web in their learning log.

The morning cruises along, and soon it is time for their reading block. Virginia is excited to get started with three guided reading groups. She has found a wonderful multilevel text that she wants to take them through. *Robots Slither!* (Hunter 2004) will be great for these groups. One group will love the rhyming story and be able to read all the words. The second group will enjoy the text that talks about different types of robots. The third group will be able to read the two different types of text in the book. *I know the book will appeal to the boys and girls in the group,* she thinks as she watches the different groups get ready.

One group is getting organized for their readers' theater performance. *Isn't that coming up next week?* Virginia thinks to herself. *I'll have to check with the retirement home to see if it's OK that we bring chocolate chip cookies for the audience. They'll love the performances, I think.* She watches as the group members pore over their scripts, making sure each member understands his or her part. The other group has moved to the inquiry station. She is thankful she was able to get help from the media specialist in gathering a number of resources related to the winter Olympics. Individuals and partners have all selected different winter sports and are reading voraciously as they take notes on their information webs and share what they are learning about their sports with other students in the room. They move quickly, taking notes from nonfiction books, sports magazines, catalogs, and the Internet. Happy with the level of engagement of her students, Virginia begins to work with her first guided reading group. The hour zips by as the three groups rotate through the activities. By the end, all students have read *Robots Slither!,* practiced their readers' theater performance, and worked on their inquiry projects. *Why can't every day go this smoothly?* she wonders.

During the last fifteen minutes of the reading block, the entire class participates in SSR. With the book *Down the Rabbit Hole* (Abrahams 2005) in front of her, Virginia glances around the room. She thinks after a quick glance around the room, *I am amazed at how many different things my kids are reading.* She notices that one of her students, Sarah, has the reading anthology for reading time. She makes a mental note to ask Sarah if she chose that book because of the stories in the section about mysteries. Sarah had been excited about the Encyclopedia Brown books Virginia had introduced them to the week before. *I wonder if she'd like the Two-Minute Mysteries books too,* she thinks.

Reading time finishes up. Virginia invites students to pair-share their responses to what they have been reading and the class is ready to transition into their writing activity. Virginia is a bit nervous for this new activity. She is going to try to make a reading-writing connection with the use of a cyber text. She is curious as to whether students will make the connection between using text-messaging language and Standard English. It is a long shot, but it is worth a try. She has seen so many kids around using their phones to send messages. She thinks it will be a fun new activity.

Reader Response Guide

Discussion Questions	Response
What stood out for you in the vignette?	
What is Virginia's definition of a reader?	
What is Virginia's definition of a text?	
What is Virginia's definition of a context?	
What is *your* definition of a reader?	
What is *your* definition of a text?	
What is *your* definition of a context?	
As far as your answers go, how would they show themselves in your classroom?	

Self-Assessment Guide

Question	Response
1. What texts do I currently use in my reading program?	
a. What texts do I currently use during read-aloud?	
b. What texts do I currently use during shared reading?	
c. What texts do I currently use during guided reading?	
d. What texts do I currently let my students use during independent reading?	
2. What texts could I add to my reading program?	
a. What texts could I add to my read-alouds?	
b. What texts could I add to my shared reading?	

c. What texts could I add to my guided reading?	
d. What texts could I add for my students to read during independent reading?	

Abrahams, P. 2005. *Down the Rabbit Hole*. New York: Laura Geringer.

Adler, D. 1981. *Cam Jansen and the Mystery of the Television Dog*. New York: Scholastic.

Adoff, A. 1989. *Chocolate Dreams: Poems*. New York: Lothrop, Lee & Shepard.

Adoff, J. 2002. *The Song Shoots Out of My Mouth: A Celebration of Music*. New York: Dutton.

Ahlberg, A., and J. Ahlberg. 1986. *The Jolly Postman*. Boston: Little, Brown.

Allen, S., and J. Lindaman. 2003. *Read Anything Good Lately?* Minneapolis: Millbrook.

Anderson, M. T. 2004. *Feed*. Cambridge, MA: Candlewick.

Arnold, K. 2005. *Elephants Can Paint, Too!* New York: Simon and Schuster.

Arnold, T. 1997. *Parts*. New York: Dial Books for Young Readers.

———. 2001. *More Parts*. New York: Dial Books for Young Readers.

———. 2004. *Even More Parts*. New York: Dial Books for Young Readers.

Auch, M. J., and H. Auch. 2003. *Souperchicken*. New York: Holiday House.

Avi. 2005. *Poppy's Return*. New York: Harper Collins.

Baker, J. 2004. *Home*. New York: Greenwillow.

Baker, O. 1985. *Where the Buffaloes Begin*. New York: Puffin.

Balor, B. 1986. *Hawk, I'm Your Brother*. New York: Aladdin.

Bandoux, A. 2001. *The Destiny of Linus Hoppe*. New York: Delacorte.

Barrett, R. 2005. *The Nutty News*. New York: Knopf.

Bartoletti, S. C. 1999. *Growing Up in Coal Country*. Boston: Houghton Mifflin.

Bateman, C. 2005. *Bring Me the Head of Oliver Plunkett*. New York: Delacorte.

Bedard, M. 1992. *Emily*. New York: Doubleday Books for Young Readers.

Bennett Hopkins, L. 2005. *Oh, No! Where Are My Pants? And Other Disaster Poems*. New York: HarperCollins.

Blume, J. 1991. *Deenie*. New York: Laurel Leaf.

Brashares, A. 2003. *The Second Summer of Sisterhood*. New York: Delacorte.

Brooks Wallace, B. 2003. *The Perils of Peppermint*. New York: Atheneum.

Brown, K. 2001. *What's the Time, Grandma Wolf?* Atlanta: Peachtree.

Burchett, J., and S. Vogler. 2005. *The Lady Grace Mysteries: Deception*. New York: Delacorte.

Byar, B. 1977. *Pinballs.* New York: Harper & Row.

Carlson, L. 1999. *You're On! Seven Plays in English and Spanish.* New York: Morrow Junior.

Catalano, D. 1998. *Frog Went A-Courting.* Honesdale, PA: Boyds Mills.

Cave, K. 2002. *One Child, One Seed: A South African Counting Book.* New York: Henry Holt.

Chandler Warner, G. 1989. *The Boxcar Children: Surprise Island.* Morton Grove, IL: Albert Whitman.

Cherry, L. 1994. *The Armadillo from Armarillo.* San Diego: Harcourt Brace.

Cole, J. 1999. *The Magic School Bus Explores the Senses.* New York: Scholastic.

Coleman, M. 1997. *Internet Detectives: Speed Surf.* New York: Skylark.

Collard, S. III. 2002. *Beaks!* Watertown, MA: Charlesbridge.

———. 2005. *A Platypus, Probably.* Watertown, MA: Charlesbridge.

Coville, B. 1993. *Aliens Ate My Homework.* New York: Aladdin.

Creech, S. 2001. *A Fine, Fine School.* New York: Joanna Cotler/HarperCollins.

———. 2003. *Love That Dog.* New York: HarperTrophy.

———. 2005a. *Heartbeat.* New York: HarperTrophy.

———. 2005b. *Replay.* New York: Joanna Cotler/HarperCollins.

Crilley, M. 2005. *Akiko: The Training Master.* New York: Delacorte.

Cronin, D. 2003. *Diary of a Worm.* New York: Joanna Cotler.

———. 2005. *Diary of a Spider.* New York: Joanna Cotler.

Curtis, C. P. 2005. *Flint Future Detectives: Mr. Chickee's Funny Money.* New York: Wendy Lamb.

Danneberg, J. 2003. *First Year Letters.* Watertown, MA: Charlesbridge.

Davies, N. 2005. *Ice Bear: In the Steps of the Polar Bear.* Cambridge, MA: Candlewick.

Davis Jones, M. 2003. *Pigs Rock.* New York: Viking.

Demarest, C. 2005. *Alpha, Bravo, Charlie: The Military Alphabet.* New York: Simon and Schuster.

DiCamillo, K. 2005. *Mercy Watson to the Rescue.* Cambridge, MA: Candlewick.

Diggory Shields, C. 1998. *Lunch Money and Other Poems About School.* New York: Puffin.

———. 2003. *Almost Late for School: And More School Poems.* New York: Dutton.

Dodd, E. 2000. *Dog's A B C: A Silly Story About the Alphabet.* New York: Dutton.

Duey, K. 2003. *The Unicorn's Secret: The Journey Home.* New York: Aladdin.

Euwer Wolff, V. 1994. *Make Lemonade.* New York: Scholastic.

Faulkner, K. 2003. *Big Bugs! Giant Creepy Crawly Pop-Ups.* New York: Scholastic.

Fisher, A. 1980. *Out in the Dark and Daylight.* New York: Harper & Row.

Fleischman, P. 1989. *I Am Phoenix: Poems for Two Voices.* New York: HarperTrophy.

———. 1992. *Joyful Noise: Poems for Two Voices.* New York: HarperTrophy.

———. 2000. *Big Talk: Poems for Four Voices.* Cambridge, MA: Candlewick.

———. 2003. *Seek.* Chicago: Cricket.

Fleischman, S. 1962. *Mr. Mysterious and Company.* Boston: Little, Brown.

———. 1966. *Chancy and the Grand Rascal.* Boston: Little, Brown.

———. 1978. *Humbug Mountain.* Boston: Little, Brown.

———. 1998. *Bandit's Moon.* New York: Greenwillow.

Fletcher, S. 1997. *The Dragon Chronicles: Dragon's Milk*. New York: Aladdin.

Flor Ada, A. 1997. *Dear Peter Rabbit*. New York: Aladdin.

———. 1998. *Yours Truly, Goldilocks*. New York: Aladdin.

———. 2001. *With Love, Little Red Hen*. New York: Aladdin.

Florian, D. 2003. *Bow Wow, Meow Meow: It's Rhyming Cats and Dogs*. New York: Harcourt Children's.

Freeman, R. 1998. *Kids at Work: Lewis Hine and the Crusade Against Child Labor*. New York: Clarion.

Furlong, M. 1989. *Wise Child Trilogy: Wise Child*. New York: Random House.

Giff, P. R. 1986. *Kids of Polk Street School: Sunnyside Up*. New York: Yearling.

Glori, D. 2005. *Pure Dead Trouble*. New York: Knopf.

Gobel, P. 1993. *The Girl Who Loved Wild Horses*. New York: Aladdin.

Greenfield, E. 1978. *Honey, I Love, and Other Love Poems*. New York: Crowell.

Grimes, N. 2002. *Bronx Masquerade*. New York: Dial.

Helldorfer, M. C. 2004. *Got to Dance*. New York: Doubleday.

Henkes, K. 1988. *Chester's Way*. New York: Greenwillow.

———. 1996. *Lilly's Purple Plastic Purse*. New York: Greenwillow.

———. 2006. *Lilly's Big Day*. New York: Greenwillow.

Hesse, K. 1999. *Out of the Dust*. New York: Scholastic.

Hirschi, R. 1997. *Faces in the Forest*. New York: Penguin.

Hoberman, M. A. 2005. *You Read to Me, I'll Read to You: Very Short Mother Goose Tales to Read Together*. New York: Megan Tingley.

Hunter, R. 2004. *Robots Slither!* New York: Putnam.

James, S. 1991. *Dear Mr. Blueberry*. New York: Aladdin.

Janeczko, P. 2001. *A Poke in the Eye: A Collection of Concrete Poems*. Cambridge: MA: Candlewick.

———. 2005. *A Kick in the Head: An Everyday Guide to Poetic Forms*. Cambridge: MA: Candlewick.

Jenkins, M. 2003. *Grandma Elephant's in Charge*. Cambridge, MA: Candlewick.

Juster, N. 1961. *The Phantom Tollbooth*. New York: Random House.

Katz, A. 2001. *Take Me Out of the Bathtub and Other Silly, Dilly Songs*. New York: Margaret K. McElderry.

———. 2003. *I'm Still Here in the Bathtub: Brand New Silly Dilly Songs*. New York: Margaret K. McElderry.

——— A. 2005. *Where Did They Hide My Presents? Silly Dilly Christmas Songs*. New York: Margaret K. McElderry.

Keller, L. 2003. *Arnie the Doughnut*. New York: Henry Holt.

Kitamura, S. 2002. *Comic Adventure of Boots*. New York: Farrar, Straus, Giroux.

Korman, G. 1984. *No Coins Please*. New York: Scholastic.

———. 1989. *Radio Fifth Grade*. New York: Scholastic.

———. 1996. *The Chicken Doesn't Skate*. New York: Scholastic.

———. 2002a. *Everest: The Summit*. New York: Scholastic.

———. 2002b. *No More Dead Dogs*. New York: Hyperion.

———. 2002c. *Son of the Mob*. New York: Hyperion.

———. 2003. *Dive: The Discovery*. New York: Scholastic.

———. 2005. *On the Run: The Stowaway Solution*. New York: Scholastic.

Kotzwinkle, W., and G. Murray. 2001. *Walter the Farting Dog*. Berkeley, CA: Frog.

Kranking, K. 2003. *The Ocean Is. . . .* New York: Henry Holt.

Lansky, B. 2002. *Funny Little Poems for Funny Little People*. New York: Meadowbrook.

Lear, E. 1996. *The Owl and the Pussycat*. New York: Atheneum.

Lester, H. 1988. *Tacky the Penguin*. Boston: Houghton Mifflin.

———. 2005. *Tacky and the Winter Games*. Boston: Houghton Mifflin.

Lewis, C. S. 2000. *The Lion, the Witch, and the Wardrobe*. New York: HarperTrophy.

Linn, G. 2004. *Fortune Cookie Fortunes*. New York: Knopf.

Lowry, L. 1990. *Number the Stars*. Boston: Houghton Mifflin.

Lum, K. 1998. *What! Cried Granny: An Almost Bedtime Story*. New York: Dial.

MacArthur, N. 1988. *The Plant That Ate Dirty Gym Socks*. New York: Avon.

Manes, S. 1991. *Make Four Million Dollars by Next Thursday*. New York: Bantam Doubleday Dell Books for Young Readers.

———. 1995. *An Almost Perfect Game*. New York: Scholastic.

———. 1996. *Be a Perfect Person in Just Three Days*. New York: Bantam Doubleday Dell Books for Young Readers.

Mannis, C. 2002. *One Leaf Rides the Wind*. New York: Penguin.

———. 2003. *The Queen's Progress: An Elizabethan Alphabet*. New York: Penguin.

Mason, S. 2003. *The Quigleys at Large*. New York: David Fickling.

McCord, D. 1977. *One at a Time*. Boston: Little, Brown.

McElroy, L. 2005. *Love, Lizzie: Letters to a Military Mom*. Morton Grove, IL: Albert Whitman.

Medaugh, S. 2001. *Martha the Talking Dog*. New York: Merrymakers.

Melmed, L. 2005. *New York, New York: The Big Apple from A to Z*. New York: HarperCollins.

Mercado, N., ed. 2005. *Every Man for Himself: Ten Short Stories About Being a Guy*. New York: Dial.

Moss, J. 1989. *The Butterfly Jar*. New York: Bantam.

———. 1991. *The Other Side of the Door*. New York: Bantam.

Moss, M. 2003. *Max's Logbook*. New York: Scholastic.

Mugford, S. 2005. *Sharks and Other Dangers of the Deep*. New York: St. Martin's.

Muntean, M. 2006. *Do Not Open This Book!* New York: Scholastic.

Myers, W. D. 2001. *Monster*. New York: Amistad.

———. 2004a. *Here in Harlem: Poems in Many Voices*. New York: Holiday House.

———. 2004b. *Shooter*. New York: Amistad.

Myracle, L. 2005. *ttyl*. New York: Harry N. Abrams.

———. 2006. *ttfn*. New York: Amulet.

Nelson, M. 2001. *Carver: A Life in Poems*. Asheville, NC: Front Street.

Pallotta, J. 2005. *Ocean Counting*. Watertown, MA: Charlesbridge

Parish, P. 2005. *Amelia Bedelia Rocket Scientist*. New York: Greenwillow.

Park, B. 1999. *Junie B. Jones and the Mushy Gushy Valentine*. New York: Random House.

Parker, T. 2005. *Sienna's Scrapbook*. San Francisco: Chronicle.

Parr, T. 2005. *Reading Makes You Feel Good*. Boston: Little, Brown.

Paterson, K. 1992. *Lyddie*. New York: Puffin.

Paulson, G. 2003. *Brian's Hunt*. New York: Wendy Lamb.

Perkins, L. R. 2005. *Criss Cross*. New York: Greenwillow.

Pilkey, D. 1994. *Dog Breath.* New York: Blue Sky.

———. 1999. *Captain Underpants and the Attack of the Talking Toilets.* New York: Scholastic.

Pope Osborne, M. 2002. *Magic Tree House: Good Morning Gorilla.* New York: Random House.

Reilly Giff, P. 1992. *Show Time at the Polk Street School: Plays You Can Do Yourself or in the Classroom.* New York: Delacorte.

Reynolds Naylor, P. 2000. *Shiloh.* New York: Aladdin.

———. 2001. *The Boys: A Traitor Among the Boys.* New York: Random House.

———. 2002. *The Girls: A Spy Among the Girls.* New York: Yearling.

Rowe, J. 2005. *Moondog.* New York: Penguin.

Rowling, J. K. 2005. *Harry Potter and the Half-Blood Prince.* New York: Scholastic.

Roy, R. 2004. *A to Z Mysteries: The White Wolf.* New York: Random House.

Rylant, C. 1996. *Henry and Mudge in Puddle Trouble.* New York: Aladdin.

———. 2005. *Mr. Putter and Tabby Write the Book.* New York: Harcourt.

Sachar, L. 2004. *Sideways Stories from Wayside School.* New York: HarperTrophy.

Scieszka, J. 1994. *The Frog Prince: Continued.* New York: Puffin.

———. 1996. *The True Story of the Three Little Pigs.* New York: Puffin.

———. 1998. *Time Warp Trio: Summer Reading Is Killing Me.* New York: Viking.

Scieszka, J., and L. Smith. 2004. *Science Verse.* New York: Viking Juvenile.

Shannon, D. 2006. *Good Boy, Fergus!* New York: Scholastic.

Shapiro, K. J. 2005. *Because I Could Not Stop My Bike and Other Poems.* Watertown, MA: Charlesbridge.

Silverstein, S. 1974. *Where the Sidewalk Ends.* New York: HarperCollins.

———. 1981. *A Light in the Attic.* New York: HarperCollins.

Sis, P. 2004. *The Train of the States.* New York: Greenwillow.

Snicket, L. 1999. *A Series of Unfortunate Events: The Bad Beginning.* New York: HarperCollins.

Sobol, D. 1967. *Two-Minute Mysteries.* New York: Scholastic.

———. 2003. *Encyclopedia Brown and the Case of the Jumping Frogs.* New York: Delacorte.

Soto, G. 1997. *Novio Boy.* New York: Harcourt.

Spiegelman, A., and F. Mouly. 2003. *"It Was a Dark and Silly Night."* New York: HarperCollins.

Stewart, P., and C. Riddle. 2002. *The Edge Chronicles: The Last of the Sky Pirates.* New York: David Fickling.

Stine, R. L. 2006. *Don't Close Your Eyes.* New York: Delacorte.

Stone, J. 2005. *The Five Ancestors: Monkey.* New York: Random House.

Sullivan, G. 2005. *Built to Last: Building America's Amazing Bridges, Dams, Tunnels, and Skyscrapers.* New York: Scholastic.

Sullivan, S. 2005. *Dear Baby: Letters from Your Big Brothers.* Cambridge, MA: Candlewick.

Tainish, R., and S. Mugford. 2004a. *Dinosaur Picture Pops.* New York: St. Martin's.

———. 2004b. *Jungle.* New York: St. Martin's.

———. 2004c. *Machines.* New York: St. Martin's.

Usher, M. 2005. *Wise Guy: The Life and Philosophy of Socrates.* New York: Farrar, Straus, Giroux.

Van Draanen, W. 2004. *Sammy Keyes and the Dead Giveaway.* New York: Knopf.

———. 2005. *Shredderman: Secret Identity.* New York: Knopf.

Varon, S. 2006. *Chicken and Cat.* New York: Scholastic.

Weitzman, D. 2005. *A Subway for New York.* New York: Farrar, Straus, Giroux.

Willems, M. 2003. *Don't Let the Pigeon Drive the Bus.* New York: Hyperion.

———. 2004. *The Pigeon Finds a Hot Dog.* New York: Hyperion.

Wolf, A. 2003. *The Blood Hungry Spleen and Other Poems About Our Parts.* Cambridge, MA: Candlewick.

Woodson, J. 2004. *Locomotion.* New York: G. P. Putnam's Sons.

Wrede, P. 1990. *The Enchanted Forest Chronicles: Dealing with Dragon.* San Diego: Magic Carpet.

Yolen, J. 2002. *Snow, Snow: Winter Poems for Children.* Honesdale, PA: Boyds Mills.

———. 2003. *Least Things: Poems About Small Natures.* Honesdale, PA: Boyds Mills.

Alexander, S. 2003. *Small Plays for Special Days.* New York: Clarion.

Allington, R. 1983. "The Reading Instruction Provided Readers of Differing Reader Ability." *Elementary School Journal* 83: 255–65.

———. 2006. *What Struggling Readers Really Need.* 2d ed. New York: Allyn and Bacon.

Armbruster, B. 1984. "The Problem of Inconsiderate Text." In *Comprehension Instruction: Perspectives and Suggestions,* ed. G. Duffy, L. Roehler, and J. Mason, 202–17. New York: Longman.

Backes, A. 1995. "On Sponsorship of Real Language Activities." *English Journal* 84 (7): 17–20.

Baker, L., and A. Wigfield. 1999. "Dimensions of Children's Motivation for Reading and Their Relations to Reading Activity and Achievement." *Reading Research Quarterly* 34: 452–77.

Barches, S. 2004. *Judge for Yourself: Famous American Trials for Readers Theatre.* Westport, CT: Teacher Ideas.

Baumann, J. F., J. V. Hoffman, J. Moon, and A. M. Duffy-Hester. 1998. "Where Are Teachers' Voices in the Phonics/Whole Language Debate? Results from a Survey of U.S. Elementary Classroom Teachers." *The Reading Teacher* 51: 636–50.

Braunger, J., and J. P. Lewis. 2006. *Building a Knowledge Base in Reading.* 2d ed. Newark, DE: International Reading Association.

Bruchac, J. 2000. *Pushing Up the Sky: Seven Native American Plays for Children.* New York: Dial.

Burgstahler, S., and L. Utterback. 2000. *New Kids on the Net: Internet Activities in Elementary Language Arts.* Boston: Allyn and Bacon.

Buss, K., and L. Karnowski. 2000. *Reading and Writing Literary Genres.* Newark, DE: International Reading Association.

———. 2002. *Reading and Writing Nonfiction Genres.* Newark, DE: International Reading Association.

Calkins, L. 1986. *The Art of Teaching Writing.* Portsmouth, NH: Heinemann.

Cary, S. 2004. *Going Graphic: Comics at Work in the Multilingual Classroom.* Portsmouth, NH: Heinemann.

Certo, J. 2004. "Cold Plums and the Old Men in the Water: Let Children Read and Write 'Great' Poetry." *Reading Teacher* 58 (November): 266–71.

Chandler-Olcott, K., and D. Mahar. 2001. "Considering Genre in the Digital Literacy Classroom." Retrieved February 17, 2006, from *Reading Online,* www.readingonline.org.

Clay, M. 1991. "Introducing a New Storybook to Young Readers." *The Reading Teacher* 45 (4): 264–73.

Cohen, E. 1994. *Designing Groupwork: Strategies for the Heterogeneous Classroom.* New York: Teachers College Press.

Coiro, J. 2003. "Reading Comprehension on the Internet: Expanding Our Understanding of Reading Comprehension to Encompass New Literacies." *The Reading Teacher* 56: 458–64.

Danielson, K., and J. Harrington. 2005. "From *The Popcorn Book* to *Popcorn:* Multigenre Children's Books." *Reading Horizons* 46 (1): 46–61.

Decker, N. 1992. "Reflections on Change: He Wouldn't Trade for Easier Wishes." *WSRA Journal* 36: 33–34.

Duke, N. 2000. "3.6 Minutes Per Day: The Scarcity of Informational Texts in First Grade." *Reading Research Quarterly* 35 (2): 202–24.

Duke, N., and P. D. Pearson. 2002. "Effective Practices for Developing Reading Comprehension." In *What Research Has to Say About Reading Instruction,* 3d ed., ed. A. E. Farstrup and S. J. Samuels, 205–42. Newark, DE: International Reading Association.

Dymock, S. 2005. "Teaching Expository Text Structure Awareness." *The Reading Teacher* 59: 177–82.

Dzaldo, B., and S. Peterson. 2005. "Book Leveling and Readers." *The Reading Teacher* 59 (3): 222–29.

Edfeldt, A. 1990. "Teaching Analytical Reading with Newspapers as Sole Reading Texts." *Research Bulletins* 14 (2): 1–23.

Edmunds, K., and K. Bauserman. 2006. "What Teachers Can Learn About Reading Motivation Through Conversations with Children." *The Reading Teacher* 59 (5): 414–24.

El-Hindi, A. 1998. "Beyond Classroom Boundaries: Constructivist Teaching with the Internet." *The Reading Teacher* 51: 694–700.

Engelhardt, Tom. 1991. "Reading May Be Harmful to Your Kids." *Harper's* 282: 55–62.

Fawson, P., and R. Reutzel. 2000. "But I Only Have a Basal: Guided Reading in the Early Grades." *The Reading Teacher* 53: 84–97.

Fielding, L., and C. Roller. 1992. "Making Difficult Books Accessible and Easy Books Acceptable." *The Reading Teacher* 45: 678–85.

Ford, M. P. 2004. "Riding in the Cars with Boys: Yu-Gi-Oh, Game Boy, and Teachable Moments." *Wisconsin State Reading Association Journal* 44: 60–63.

Ford, M., and M. Opitz. 2002. "Using Centers to Engage Children During Guided Reading Time: Intensifying Learning Experiences Away from the Teacher." *The Reading Teacher* 55 (8): 710–17.

Fredericks, A. 2002. *Science Fiction Readers Theatre.* Westport, CT: Teacher Ideas.

Gambrell, L. B. 1992. "Elementary School Literacy Instruction: Changes and Challenges." In *Elementary School Literacy: Critical Issues,* ed. M. J. Dreher and W. H. Slater, 227–39. Norwood, MA: Christopher Gordon.

Gunning, T. 2003. *Creating Literacy Instruction for All Children*. Boston: Allyn and Bacon.

Guthrie, J., and E. Anderson. 1999. "Engagement in Reading." In *Engaged Reading: Processes, Practices, and Policy Implications*, ed. J. Guthrie and D. Alverman, 17–45. New York: Teachers College Press.

Hall, K. M., B. L. Sabey, and M. McClellan. 2005. "Expository Text Comprehension: Helping Primary-Grade Teachers Use Expository Texts to Full Advantage." *Reading Psychology* 26: 211–34.

Harris, T. L., and R. E. Hodges. 1995. *The Literacy Dictionary: The Vocabulary of Reading and Writing*. Newark, DE: International Reading Association.

Harste, J. 1998. "A Model of Difference." *The Council Chronicle* (Sept.).

Huck, C., B. Kiefer, S. Hepler, and J. Hickman. 2005. *Children's Literature in the Elementary School*. New York: McGraw Hill.

International Reading Association (IRA). 2001. *Integrating Literacy and Technology in the Curriculum: A Position Statement*. Newark, DE: International Reading Association. Retrieved February 21, 2006, from www.reading.org/positions/technology.html.

International Reading Association Board of Directors. 1999. *Providing Books and Other Print Materials for Classroom and School Libraries: A Position Statement of the International Reading Association*. Newark, DE: International Reading Association.

Jacobs, J., and M. Tunnell. 2004. *Children's Literature, Briefly*. 3d ed. Upper Saddle River, NJ: Pearson/Merrill/Prentice Hall.

Janeczko, P. 2003. *Opening a Door: Reading Poetry in the Middle School Classroom*. New York: Scholastic.

Jenkins, D. 2004. *Just Deal with It! Funny Readers Theatre for Life's Not-So-Funny Moments*. Westport, CT: Teacher Ideas.

Kamil, M. L., H. S. Kim, and D. M. Lane. 2004. "Electronic Text in the Classroom." In *The Texts in Elementary Classrooms*, ed. J. V. Hoffman and D. L. Schallert, 157–93. Mahwah, NJ: Lawrence Erlbaum.

Kamil, M. L., and D. M. Lane. 1998. "Researching the Relationship Between Technology and Literacy: An Agenda for the 21st Century." In *Handbook of Literacy Technology: Transformations in a Post-Typographic World,* ed. D. Reinking, M. McKenna, L. Labbo, and R. Keifer, 323–41. Mahwah, NJ: Erlbaum.

Kantor, R., T. Anderson, and B. Armbruster. 1983. "How Are Children's Textbooks Inconsiderate? Or of Flyswatters and Alfa." *Journal of Curriculum Study* 15 (1): 61–72.

Karchmer, R. A., M. H. Mallette, J. Kara-Soteriou, and D. J. Leu, eds. 2005. *Innovative Approaches to Literacy Education: Using the Internet to Support New Literacies*. Newark, DE: International Reading Association.

Keene, E., and S. Zimmerman. 1997. *Mosaic of Thought: Teaching Comprehension in a Reader's Workshop*. Portsmouth, NH: Heinemann.

Kismaric, C., and M. Heiferman. 1996. *Growing up with Dick and Jane: Learning and Living the American Dream*. New York: Harper.

Kohn, A. 1996. *Beyond Discipline: From Compliance to Community*. Alexandria, VA: Association for Supervision and Curriculum Development.

Kornfeld, J., and G. Leyden. 2005. "Acting Out: Literature, Drama, and Connecting with History." *The Reading Teacher* 59: 230–38.

Krashen, S. 2004. *The Power of Reading: Insights from the Research.* 2d ed. Portsmouth, NH: Heinemann.

———. 2005. "Comic Books Encourage Reading." *USA Today,* 5 May.

Kreul, M. 2005. "Connecting Technology and Literacy: A Journey from 'How Do I Turn on This Computer?' to 'My Class Is Blogging Their Book Reviews for Literature Circles.'" In *Innovative Approaches to Literacy Education: Using the Internet to Support New Literacies,* ed. R. A. Karchmer, M. H. Mallette, J. Kara-Soteriou, and D. J. Leu, 138–56. Newark, DE: International Reading Association.

Kucer, S. 2005. *Dimensions of Literacy.* 2d ed. Mahwah, NJ: Lawrence Erlbaum.

Laminack, L., and B. Bell. 2004. "Stretching the Boundaries and Blurring the Lines of Genre." *Language Arts* 81: 248–53.

Lattimer, H. 2003. *Thinking Through Genre: Units of Study in Reading and Writing Workshops 4–12.* York, ME: Stenhouse.

Leslie, L., and M. Jett-Simpson. 1997. *Authentic Literacy Assessment: An Ecological Approach.* New York: Longman.

Leu, D. Jr. 2002. "Internet Workshop: Making Time for Literacy." Retrieved February 17, 2006, from *Reading Online,* www.readingonline.org.

Leu, D. J., C. K. Kinzer, J. Coiro, and D. Cammack. 2004. "Toward a Theory of New Literacies Emerging from the Internet and Other Information and Communication Technology." In *Theoretical Models and Processes of Reading,* 5th ed., ed. R. Rudell and N. Unrau, 1570–1613. Newark, DE: International Reading Association.

Leu, D. J., M. H. Mallette, R. A. Karchmer, and J. Kara-Soteriou. 2005. "Contextualizing the New Literacies of Information and Communication Technologies in Theory, Research and Practice." In *Innovative Approaches to Literacy Education: Using the Internet to Support New Literacies,* ed. R. A. Karchmer, M. H. Mallette, J. Kara-Soteriou, and D. J. Leu, 1–10. Newark, DE: International Reading Association.

Maggio, R., ed. 1997. *Quotations in Education.* Paramus, NJ: Prentice-Hall.

Malloy, J. A., and L. B. Gambrell. 2006. "Approaching the Unavoidable: Literacy Instruction and the Internet." *The Reading Teacher* 59: 482–84.

McCann, E. 1994. *Fairy Tale Plays for Oral Reading.* North Billerica, MA: Curriculum Associates.

McKenna, M., L. Labbo, and D. Reinking. 2003. "Effective Use of Technology in Literacy Instruction." In *Best Practices in Literacy Instruction,* 2d ed., ed. L. Morrow, L. Gambrell, and M. Pressley, 307–31. New York: Guilford.

McKenna, M., D. Reinking, and L. Labbo. 1997. "Using Talking Books with Reading-Disabled Students." *Reading and Writing Quarterly* 13: 185–90.

McTaggart, J. 2005. "Using Comics and Graphic Novels to Encourage Reluctant Readers." *Reading Today* (Oct.–Nov.): 46.

Meek, M. 1988. *How Texts Teach What Readers Learn.* South Worchester, England: Thimble.

Meyer, B., and E. Rice. 1984. "The Structure of Text." In *Handbook of Reading Research,* ed. P. D. Pearson, 309–52. New York: Longman.

Mullis, I., M. Martin, E. Gonzalez, and A. Kennedy. 2003. *Progress in International Reading Literacy Study 2001 International Report: IEA's Study of Reading Literacy Achievement in Primary Schools.* Chestnut Hill, MA: Boston College.

National Council of Teachers of English. 1989. "Basal Readers and the State of American Reading Instruction: A Call to Action." *Language Arts* 66: 896–98.

Nodelman, P., and M. Reimer. 2003. *The Pleasures of Children's Literature*. Boston: Allyn and Bacon.

Norton, B. 2003. "The Motivating Power of Comic Books: Insights from Archie Comic Readers." *The Reading Teacher* 57 (2): 140–47.

Norton-Meier, L. A. 2004. "The Bumper Sticker Curriculum: Learning from Words on the Backs of Cars." *Journal of Adolescent and Adult Literacy* 48: 260–63.

Opitz, M., and M. Ford. 2001. *Reaching Readers: Flexible and Innovative Strategies for Guided Reading*. Portsmouth, NH: Heinemann.

Opitz, M., and M. Zbaracki. 2005. *Listen Hear! 25 Effective Listening Comprehension Strategies*. Portsmouth, NH: Heinemann.

Palmer, B. C., H. J. Fletcher, and B. A. Shapley. 1994. "Improving Student Reading, Writing with Newspaper-Based Instruction." *Newspaper Research Journal* 15 (2): 50–55.

Paris, S., and R. Carpenter. 2004. *The Texts in Elementary Classrooms*. New York: Guilford.

Pearson, P. D., and T. Raphael. 2003. "Toward a More Complex View of Balance in the Literacy Curriculum." In *Best Practices in Literacy Instruction*, 2d ed., ed. L. Morrow, L. Gambrell, and M. Pressley, 23–42. New York: Guilford.

Peterson, B. 1991. "Selecting Books for Beginning Readers and Children's Literature Suitable for Young Readers." In *Bridges to Literacy: Learning from Reading Recovery*, ed. D. DeFord, C. Lyons, and G. Pinnell, 119–47. Portsmouth, NH: Heinemann.

Pilgren, J. 2000. *The SSR Handbook: How to Organize and Manage a Sustained Silent Reading Program*. Portsmouth, NH: Boynton/Cook.

Pilkey, D. 1994. *Dog Breath: The Horrible Trouble with Hally Tosis*. New York: Scholastic.

Rabinowitz, P. 1987. *Before Reading: Narrative Conventions and the Politics of Interpretation*. Ithaca, NY: Cornell University Press.

Roller, C., and L. Fielding. 1992. "Making Difficult Books Accessible and Easy Books Acceptable." *The Reading Teacher* 45: 678–85.

Romano, A. 2006. "Walking a New Beat: Surfing MySpace.com Helps Cops Crack the Case." *Newsweek* (April 24).

Roser, N. L., J. V. Hoffman, and N. J. Carr. 2003. "See It Change: A Primer on the Basal Reader." In *Best Practices in Literary Instruction*, 2d ed., ed. L. M. Morrow, L. B. Gambrell, and M. Pressley, 269–86. New York: Guilford.

Ross, C. S. 1995. "If They Read Nancy Drew, So What? Series Book Readers Talk Back." *Library and Information Science Research* 17: 201–36.

Schole, R. 1985. *Textual Power: Literary Theory and the Teaching of English*. New Haven, CT: Yale University Press.

Shannon, P., and K. Goodman, eds. 1994. *Basal Readers: A Second Look*. Katonah, NY: Richard C. Owen.

Shapley, B. 2001. *Reading First NIE! A Newspaper in Education Teaching Supplement for Reading First No Child Left Behind Act of 2001*. New York: Newspaper Association of America.

Sloyer, S. 2003. *From the Page to the Stage: The Educator's Complete Guide to Readers Theatre*. Westport, CT: Teacher Ideas.

Smith, C. 2003. *Extraordinary Women from U.S. History: Readers Theatre for Grades 4–8.* Portsmouth, NH: Teacher Ideas.

Smith, F. 2004. *Understanding Reading: A Psycholinguistic Analysis of Reading and Learning to Read.* 6th ed. Mahwah, NJ: Lawrence Erlbaum.

Smith, M., and J. Wilhelm. 2002. *"Reading Don't Fix No Chevys": Literacy in the Lives of Young Men.* Portsmouth, NH: Heinemann.

Smith, N. B. [1934] 2002. *American Reading Instruction.* Newark, DE: International Reading Association.

Solomon, G. 2002. "Digital Equity: It's Not Just About Access Anymore." *Technology and Learning* 22: 18–26.

Stoll, D., ed. 1997. *Magazines for Kids and Teens.* Rev. ed. Glassboro, NJ: Educational Press Association of America; Newark, DE: International Reading Association.

Strop, J. 2005. "Integrating Literacy and Content Area Learning." Paper presented at the Wisconsin State Reading Association Convention, Milwaukee.

Strop, J., H. Dionne, and R. Kuhnen. 2003. "Traveling Through Text Sets to Advanced Comprehension." Paper presented at the Secondary Reading League's Twenty-Seventh Day of Reading, Illinois Reading Council, Tinley Park Convention Center, November.

Stroud, J. 1995. "Building a Foundation for Literacy." *Early Childhood Education Journal* 23: 9–13.

Sweet, A. P., and C. Snow, eds. 2003. *Rethinking Reading Comprehension.* New York: Guilford.

Turner, J. 1995. "The Influence of Classroom Contexts on Young Children's Motivation for Literacy." *Reading Research Quarterly* 30: 410–41.

Wigfield, A. 2000. "Facilitating Children's Reading Motivation." In *Engaging Young Readers,* ed. L. Baker, M. Dreher, and J. Guthrie, 140–58. New York: Guilford.

Wiliams, J. P. 2005. "Instruction in Reading Comprehension for Primary-Grade Students: A Focus on Text Structure." *The Journal of Special Education* 39 (1): 6–18.

Wolf, J. 2002. *Cinderella Outgrows the Glass Slipper and Other Zany Fractured Fairy Tale Plays.* New York: Scholastic Professional.

Worthy, J. 2005. *Readers Theatre for Building Fluency.* New York: Scholastic.

Worthy, J., and K. Prater. 2002. "'I Thought About It All Night': Readers Theatre for Reading Fluency and Motivation." *The Reading Teacher* 56: 294–97.

Xu, S., R. S. Perkins, and L. O. Zurich. 2005. *Trading Cards to Comic Strips: Popular Culture Texts and Literacy Learning in Grades K–8.* Newark, DE: International Reading Association.

Zbaracki, M. 2003. "A Descriptive Study of How Humorous Children's Literature Serves to Engage Children in Reading." Ph.D. diss., Ohio State University, Columbus.